TRAINING YOUR PET FERRET

2nd Edition

Gerry Bucsis
Barbara Somerville

Dedication

This book is dedicated to Patch and Gabby, the little furballs who made it all possible. Also, to Seto . . . a much-loved fuzzy whose memory lives on in the photos in this book.

Note of Warning

This book deals with the keeping and training of ferrets as pets. In working with these animals, you may occasionally sustain scratches or bites. Administer first aid immediately, and seek medical attention if necessary.

Ferrets must be watched carefully during the necessary and regular exercise periods in the house. To avoid life-threatening accidents, be particularly careful that your pet does not gnaw on rubber, foam, latex, sponge, or electrical cords.

Ferrets can be carriers of serious or even life-threatening diseases that are easily spread to other ferrets. Be cautious before exposing your ferret(s) to other ferrets, or to products and surfaces that other ferrets have used. If your ferret shows any sign of illness, be sure to visit your veterinarian.

All inquiries should be addressed to:
Barron's Educational Series, Inc.
250 Wireless Boulevard
Hauppauge, New York 11788
www.barronseduc.com

ISBN-13: 978-0-7641-4223-9
ISBN-10: 0-7641-4223-2
Library of Congress Catalog Card No. 2009933080

Printed in China
9 8 7 6 5 4 3 2 1

Acknowledgments

Special thanks to:

- Our families for their support, understanding, and encouragement.
- Our friends—Jane Panagabko (Sammy); Taryn Philp and John Campbell (Link, Remy, Seto); Anna and George (Cleo and Sassy)—who allowed their ferrets to be photographed.
- The following individuals and companies for their help and cooperation:
  - Jason Casto, Super Pet, Pets International
  - Ron Leavens, Pet Valu, Fonthill, ON
  - Marshall Pet Products, Inc.
  - Rolf C. Hagen, Inc.
- Our editor, Anna Damaskos, for expert assistance and unfailing good humor
- Cover photo, courtesy of Gerry Bucsis and Barbara Somerville; inside-front cover, courtesy of Gerry Bucsis and Barbara Somerville; inside-back cover, courtesy of Gerry Bucsis and Barbara Somerville; back cover, courtesy of Gerry Bucsis and Barbara Somerville
- Photos on the following pages are courtesy of Marshall Pet Products, Inc.: 1, 13, 20, 25, 28, 62, 70 (bottom), 74, 75, and 101.
- Products on the following pages are courtesy of Marshall Pet Products, Inc.: 6, 33 (top), 34, and 76.
- Products on the following pages are courtesy of Rolf C. Hagen, Inc.: 7, 45, and 71.
- Products on the following pages are courtesy of Super Pet, Pets International, Inc.: viii, x, 2, 12, 14, 21, 22, 31, 33 (bottom), 37, 41, 48, 55, 56, 57, 61, 69, 82, and 91.

Contents

Introduction

Can you handle a bundle of energy? Are you looking for a pet that will provide hours of fun for the whole family? Are you prepared for instant attention wherever you go? Congratulations! You've made the perfect choice. Ferrets are wonderful pets and will reward you with years of fun. They are playful, lovable, endearing, and intelligent.

They are, however, different from other house pets and need a special approach when it comes to training. Ferrets are much more inquisitive and resourceful than the average cat or dog. They are constantly on the go when awake and can get into things that Tabby wouldn't even dream of! If you go out and leave your cat alone, Tabby will snooze on the sofa. If you leave your ferret on the loose, the little rascal will ransack the kitchen cupboards.

And, if you think your ferret can be trained like Fido, think again. Fido will be perfectly happy to perform for a "Good boy, well done!" Praise alone satisfies man's best friend, but it won't register with your ferret.

So, how do you train this free-roaming, curious bundle of energy? You won't find ferret obedience classes in the Yellow Pages and none of the available ferret care guides offers a complete training program. Consequently, owners have had to glean information from a variety of sources such as veterinarians, other owners, breeders, ferret organizations, friendly pet shop staff, and the Internet. Often, training has been a matter of trial and error (mostly error!).

But now there is *Training Your Pet Ferret*—all you ever wanted to know about training your ferret but didn't know who to ask. This is *not* a general care guide. There are excellent books available that provide detailed information about choosing a ferret, as well as advice on health care, grooming, and breeding. In fact, every ferret owner should have a quality care guide on hand.

Training Your Pet Ferret is a training guide. In a step-by-step approach, this book outlines specific methods for teaching and reinforcing positive behavior in your ferret. It also makes suggestions on how to tackle negative behavior: in short, the A to Z of ferret training.

So now it's up to you. Have realistic expectations for your pet. Set aside some time each day for practice. Be consistent. But most important, have FUN!

Chapter One
First Things First: Preparations

Before training, there's work to do

Now that you've made the big decision to buy a ferret, you probably want to rush right out to the breeder or pet shop and bring one home. But stop! You want to start off on the right foot, don't you? After all, the little guy will be with you for many years. Taking time to prepare adequately beforehand will be time well spent. The good news is that you won't have to break the bank for the few items you need to get started. First on your list should be home sweet home.

A ferret's house is his castle

Your ferret's cage has to be his haven, a retreat where he feels safe and secure. This is where he'll play when you're out during the day. This is where he'll most likely crash between bouts of furious activity. This is where he needs to be for his own safety when you're sleeping. Left to roam unsupervised, he can get into too much mischief.

There are several types of suitable housing. A large wire cage is

Buy the largest cage you can afford . . . your ferret needs room for exercise and play.

Make your ferret's cage a comfy home with plenty of accessories.

an excellent choice. It will give your ferret a good window on the world, letting him see what's going on around him. You can jazz up the interior decor by hanging up playthings, tubes, and hammocks for a more ferret-friendly environment.

Multistory cages provide your pet(s) with lots of leg room. You can even find a few models that can be bought a section at a time as your budget allows. Some multistory cages have full-floor platforms, some have partial platforms, and some have a combination of the two. It's important to note that ferrets don't have great depth perception, and will sometimes walk right off partial platforms. To prevent this, you can make these cages safe by rigging up hammocks adjacent to the partial platforms, or by snapping in an extra platform or two.

Large ferret condos are spacious and offer upscale comfort. To add to the comfort, why not cushion any wire or plastic platforms with carpet or a fleecy cover? And while you're at it, slip any wire ramps into hockey socks to make them safer and easier for your pet to climb.

Are you planning to build your own cage? If so, make sure it's large, safe, and easy to clean. Never use painted or pressure-treated wood; the toxins could affect your ferret's health. And avoid the use of wood for flooring and platforms, as it soaks up urine and becomes unsanitary. Wire flooring can irritate or injure your ferret's foot pads, so if the cage you make or buy has wire flooring, make it comfy with a piece of linoleum or a washable carpet mat. Stay away from fringes and rubber backing, please!

Do you have an old aquarium that you'd like to convert into a ferret cage? Not a good idea! Aquariums—even the largest ones—are unsuitable for ferrets. They may look good and be within your price range, but ventilation and overheating can be a problem, especially in the summer.

When you're shopping for a ferret cage, the most important thing to remember is that ferrets need large cages. After all, the bowls, the bedding, the litter box, the hammocks, and the toys take up a lot of space. If the cage is too small, there won't be room for your ferret. Not only that, but ferrets become stressed and depressed in a small cage. Can't afford a large cage right now? Then check the Internet for used cages, or put off your pet purchase until you've saved enough money for a spacious ferret home.

Location, location, location

Find a good spot in your house for the cage and leave it there. Animals become confused if they're constantly being moved. How would you like to find your bed in the kitchen one night and in the laundry room the next? Ferrets snooze an average of 14 hours a day. They're dead to the world when they sleep, so the spot you choose for the cage doesn't have to be super quiet. On the other hand, it shouldn't be so noisy that your ferret will have difficulty settling down. Pick a location where your pet won't be disturbed by ear-splitting speakers or a deafening TV. And, to prevent your ferret from getting overheated, keep the cage out of direct sunlight and away from heating vents. Make sure, too, that it's not in the direct path of air conditioners or fans. You don't want to freeze that furball!

Bedding basics

Never use small-animal bedding for your fuzzy. Pelleted paper and wood shavings might be okay for hamsters and gerbils, but they're not suitable for ferrets. For sleeping, ferrets like to burrow into soft bedding. Ready-made ferret tubes and sleep sacks are cozy and convenient. But there's no need to purchase anything special. Just look around your house. You'll be surprised what you can come up with. Try cut-off sweatpant legs, flannel pajamas, hockey

Cut-off sweat-pants make cozy bedding.

socks, old sweatshirts, or blankets. Watch out for anything detachable that could be chewed off and swallowed. No hooks, snaps, strings, buttons, beads, or elastic. Nix anything that has small holes because your ferret could crawl through them and get stuck. Find plenty of washable bedding that can be popped in the washer when it starts to get that familiar ferret fragrance.

Occasionally a baby ferret, called a kit, might chew his cloth bedding. A swallowed piece can cause intestinal blockage. So, if your ferret is a material muncher, give him a small cardboard box or a snooze tube to curl up in.

A passing look at litter

Every cage's floor plan should include space for a litter box. Have one ready and waiting for your new pet because he won't be able to wait until you run out and find one. The ins and outs of the litter box are covered in Chapter 6.

Food for thought—a square meal

After you've set your ferret's house in order, the next important consideration is his food. If you don't provide proper nutrition for your pet, he can stuff himself and still starve. Ferrets need high-quality dry food. The protein content must be at least 36 percent, and the fat content should be between 18 and 22 percent. Most of the protein should come from animal sources such as chicken, beef, poultry by-products, and fishmeal. Avoid any food that lists corn as one of the first three ingredients. A ferret's digestive system isn't geared to process corn. It just goes right through and ends up as extra poops in the litter box.

Fortunately, there are several specially formulated ferret foods on the market that meet your pet's nutritional needs. There are also some high-quality dry kitten or cat foods that are suitable for ferrets. Whatever you buy, make sure to read the labels and check that the protein and fat levels are adequate. Canned ferret food is nutritionally balanced, but, to keep teeth and gums healthy, it should be used in conjunction with dry food. Don't use dog food or puppy chow, and stay away from bargain-basement cat, kitten, or ferret foods.

Confused? If you can't decide what should go on your ferret's menu, do an Internet search for *ferret food comparison charts*. And if you have doubts about a particular product, check with your veterinarian.

What goes in must come out. And in a ferret's case the job gets done quickly! A ferret eats often, and digests its food in three to four hours, or in the case of kits, in an hour and a half. So food and fresh water must be available at all times in the cage and in the play area for eating on the run.

Nowadays some ferret experts and owners are advocating a raw meat or whole-prey diet for ferrets. If you're interested in going this route for your pet, do your research carefully and discuss the pros and cons with your veterinarian. Of course, you can't leave raw meat in your ferret's dish all day because it will quickly spoil. And, you'll have to watch that your ferret doesn't stash any raw food, because if it grows mold or bacteria, it will make your furball sick.

Battening down the bowls

Food flying, water sloshing, ferret clucking—that rowdy little rascal strikes again! Dragging dishes, upending bowls, scattering food, and soaking bedding—what fun (for the ferret, that is)!

How can you prevent a movable feast? Invest in sturdy, tip-proof bowls. The best bets are heavy, medium-sized crockery bowls or man-made marble dishes. The trick is to find something heavy that your ferret can't nudge, drag, or flip with his nose, mouth, or paws.

For the cage, it's a good idea to buy dishes that fasten to the cage wire and are easily removed for cleaning and filling. Look for bowls that lock in place so that your ferret can't tip them over. J-shaped feeders and bin feeders are also tip-proof and have the added advantage of holding more food.

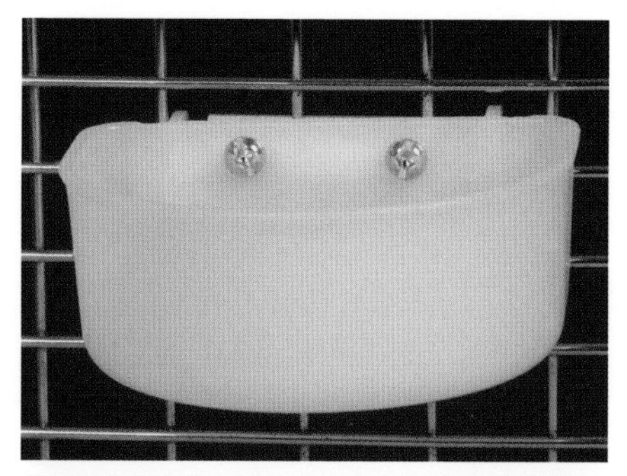

To prevent the plastic clip-on bowls in pet carriers from tipping, drill holes in them . . .

. . . and attach them to the wire door.

Does your fuzzy enjoy knocking the food and water bowls off the wire door in his travel carrier? Then you'll have to modify these snap-on bowls. How? Using two stainless steel bolts, two wing nuts, and a small, stainless steel plate with predrilled holes, secure each bowl to the cage door as illustrated in the photographs above.

Water bottles attached to the cage won't tip. But be careful to find one that doesn't drip, unless, of course, your pet has his rubber boots handy! Here's another point to remember—water bottles won't

Your fuzzy won't be able to tip or drag a bowl that's locked onto the cage wires.

work if your kit hasn't mastered the art of sipping. You might have to teach him how it's done by putting his mouth to the water tube.

Ring around the collar

A collar with a small bell attached needs to be on your shopping list. In fact, you might as well get two—one and a spare. It's not the collar that's so important; it's the bell. Any ferret, big or small, can whisk around the house in almost total silence. A bell will allow you to keep track of your pet so that you won't spend half your life looking for him. Also, when you know where he is, you'll be less likely to step on him.

If (heaven forbid!) your pet ever escapes to the great outdoors, a bell will increase your chances of finding him a hundredfold, as will a tiny I.D. tag. If you can't find an I.D. tag small enough, check with your local jewelry store about getting his bell engraved with your telephone number or use a hand engraver to do it yourself.

Buy a ferret collar or kitten collar, it doesn't matter which, as long as there's a bell attached. But look for one with some stretch or a break-away safety feature so that your tireless explorer won't choke if he gets hooked on a piece of furniture.

Given half a chance, little Houdini will slip out of his collar, so make sure that it's snug but not too tight. Check the fit periodically. Ferrets expand on their own, collars don't! Some ferrets take to a collar easily; others fight it tooth and nail and squirm out at every opportunity. What should you do with the nonconformist? Persevere. Make the collar just a teensy bit tighter. Then, every time he slips it off, put it back on and give him a treat. If he loses it, put on the spare immediately and spare yourself a lost ferret.

Rather than fitting your fuzzy with a collar and bell, you might want to opt for a harness and bell instead. A harness is safer because when it's properly fitted, your pet can't slip out of it and he won't choke if the harness gets caught on something. Make it snug, but not tight. Another good reason for buying a harness is that you can use it for walking your ferret outside on a leash, whereas you must *never, never, never* use a collar when walking your pet outdoors.

The carrot and the stick

Because training starts the very minute you pick up your pet, you'll want to have two valuable training aids on hand before bringing him home.

The first of these is a skin and coat supplement made specifically for ferrets. These supplements,

It's easier to keep track of a ferret if he's wearing a bell on his harness or collar.

which contain essential fatty acids, come in liquid form, and most ferrets absolutely love them. Offering one to your pet is like dangling a carrot in front of his nose to encourage and reinforce good behavior. If you can't find a made-for-ferrets supplement in your local pet shop, you can order it from an Internet store.

Whatever brand you choose, read the label instructions very carefully. It's important to know the maximum daily dosage and stick to it so you don't overdose your pet on vitamins. And if the daily allowance seems a bit meager for rewards, you could always dilute it half and half with olive oil or canola oil to make it go further.

The second item is a bitter spray, specially formulated for pet training. These deterrent sprays work wonders. They discourage nipping and chewing, and can be very helpful when rehabilitating a problem ferret. They aren't harmful at all; ferrets just hate the taste. A bitter spray is the only type of corrective stick to use with your pet, as physical force is never recommended in disciplining ferrets. There are many different brands on the market, and you might have to experiment a bit to find the product that works best for your particular pet.

Checking out the vets

There's one last step before you're ready to go. Call around until you find a veterinarian who is knowledgeable about and experienced with ferrets. Don't be afraid to ask questions. You'll need to arrange for an initial checkup and for canine distemper and rabies shots. Some veterinarians recommend giving the distemper and rabies shots a few weeks apart to minimize the likelihood of an adverse reaction. Ask, too, about neutering or spaying your pet if this hasn't already been done. Neutering a male reduces odor and results in a ferret with a quieter disposition. Females *must* be spayed if not kept for breeding. Otherwise, they go into prolonged heat, which results in life-threatening health problems. The pros and cons of de-scenting, if not done already, can also be discussed with the veterinarian.

Choose your veterinarian carefully. He or she will be your ferret's doctor and you'll be seeing each other at least once a year since annual booster shots and health checks are necessary for your pet's well-being. Keep in mind that a healthy ferret is a happy ferret.

Chapter Two

Bonding with Your Buddy

Getting to know you

When the pre-pet preparations are taken care of, you'll be ready for what really counts—bonding with your buddy. Bonding is all about building trust. It's about you and your ferret getting to know and love one another. Whether you choose a tiny kit or adopt an adult, bonding begins with homecoming.

Homecoming

The great moment has arrived! It's time to bring home the new addition to the family. This may well be the second move for your kit—first from the mother to the pet shop and then from the pet shop to your house. She may even have had a stopover with a distributor. So, you'll want to make this move as agreeable as possible.

For the ride home, buy a travel carrier or find a small box that you can take with you to the pet shop, shelter, or breeder. Line it with the soft bedding you intend to use in the cage. Your pet will feel more secure in the confined space of the box or travel carrier than she would on a passenger's lap, and the bedding will give her a place to hide. She won't appreciate loud music and poking fingers, but do reassure her by speaking softly.

As soon as you get home, gently place your ferret in her new cage. The sights, sounds, and smells of your house may be very frightening for her. *You* might be anxious to play

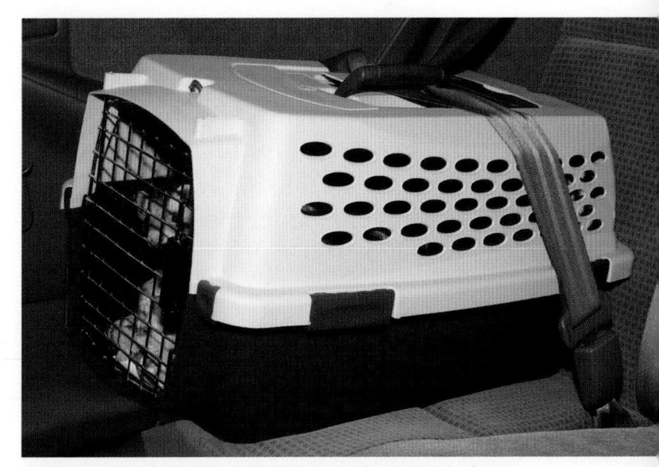

Loop a seat belt through the travel carrier to keep your ferret safe on the way to her new home.

Frequent handling makes for better bonding.

with your baby or show her to friends and neighbors. *She* will be overwhelmed. Leave her alone for a few hours to adjust to this strange, new environment. Fresh food, water, and toys will help her feel at home. Don't worry if your kit starts scratching frantically to escape. She'll settle down after a while, curl up, and sleep. When she wakes up, the fun begins!

To have is to hold

When the new arrival's up and about and has had a good sniff around her new quarters, it's time for handling session number one. You don't want to startle her, so speak quietly as you pick her up. Cradling the newcomer in your arms, stroke her fur, rub her ears, and scratch her under the chin. Massage those hind legs and tickle that tummy. Brush her with a soft pet-grooming brush as you whisper sweet nothings in her ear.

Keep in mind that a kit is a baby with lots of energy. She may not want to be handled at first, so be prepared for wriggling and jumping. Be careful, don't drop her, but handle her anyway. Don't put her down as soon as she starts wiggling. Hold her a little bit longer to show who's boss. After all, who's training whom?

Your ferret needs to learn that being held is enjoyable. So, when she's in angelic mode, cuddling close, give her a few licks of skin and coat supplement as a reward for good behavior.

How often is enough?

That's it for your first handling session. There wasn't much to it, was there? It's a snap from here on in. Just repeat the handling over and over, and over and over, and over and over, and—get the point?

So, how often is enough? Try to get in as many short socializing sessions per day as possible. Even five minutes at a time is fine. In fact, many short sessions are better than a few marathon ones. Are you busy at work or school all day? Try to find time for your ferret before going out in the mornings and as soon as you get home. Just don't expect a kit who's caged all day to cooperate miraculously at supper time!

The best way to bond with your new ferret is to handle her often—very often. *The more frequently you handle your kit, the more loving she will be as an adult.* The same holds true if you've adopted an older ferret. Frequent handling is the key to success.

Rebel on the run

If you have a little rebel with ideas of her own—mainly run, run, run—you can make things easy on yourself. Get out the secret weapon you have on hand—the skin and coat supplement. A drop or two of liquid supplement will have her licking her lips. She'll soon stop struggling when she realizes that being held equals a goodie.

Here's another trick to keep up your sleeve for those times when the kit won't cooperate. It's much easier to handle a full ferret. A hungry one will be more interested in visiting her food bowl than visiting with you.

Sometimes, though, there might be a legitimate reason for a squirmy ferret. The wiggles could mean she needs exercise. Several daily workouts in a restricted area are essential. See Chapters 4 and 5.

If she's extremely squirmy, perhaps she needs to use the litter box *right now*. Excessive fidgeting is universal ferret body language for "I gotta go!" Pop her back into the cage and try handling her again later.

Cradle your kit with both hands to keep her safe.

"Hissss" . . . what is this?

Sometimes when you go to pick up your pet, she might start hissing at you. If you're a novice owner, this can be frightening, especially when the hissing is accompanied by an arched back and bristling fur. What in the world is your ferret trying to tell you? This depends. Some ferrets are just "hissers"—hissing is their way of communicating. Other ferrets hiss when they're happy and playful, and want to roughhouse. Sometimes, ferrets hiss when they're trying to act "big" and show that they're not afraid of you. On other occasions they hiss when they're angry or upset and don't want to be picked up.

Is it time for another handling session?

When you have a new ferret, it can be difficult to figure out what your pet means by hissing. So until you know her better and can read her moods, your best plan is to speak to her in a reassuring manner and save the handling till later.

All in the family

Make handling your ferret a family affair. From Junior to Gramps, get everyone in on the act. Just don't let everybody grab for her at once. Take a low-key approach. The newcomer should feel safe and secure, not scared out of her wits.

Do kids and ferrets mix? Some breeders and veterinarians don't recommend ferrets as pets for small children. Check with your veterinarian if you have concerns. Young children should not be around a ferret, or any animal, without adult supervision. Older children need instruction on proper handling and care.

It's only natural for kids to want to hold and hug a new pet. Unfortunately, a baby ferret might have something else in mind, namely a fast getaway. You need to step in as the bonding coach. Pick a time when the kit is cooperative. Bring out the skin and coat supplement. Then sit your child down with the ferret for a short hold and treat session. This is the way to go till kid and kit get to be best buddies.

Ferret friends?

Do you already have a family ferret? Are you bringing home a friend for her? It's important to realize that ferrets often fight until one of them establishes dominance. If this happens at your house, here are a few tips to make the introductions easier.

For the first while, keep the ferrets in separate cages, but place the cages close together so that the fuzzies get used to each other's scent. After a few days, start cage swapping. Put ferret A into ferret B's cage, and vice versa, for about half an hour at a time. Next, put them together in a play area with plenty of toys around for distraction. Keep this playtime short and supervise carefully. Some fighting is to be expected, and should be allowed so they can work out a pecking order. But if the brawling gets out of hand, separate them.

Keep repeating the short playtimes. Roughhousing is okay, but if the fighting is fierce, try bathing them in the same shampoo so they smell the same. It also helps to rub a little vanilla extract on each of them to mask their individual body scents. You can also spray the back of the

Make handling . . .

. . . a family affair.

It can take time for the family ferret to accept a newcomer.

underdog's neck with a bitter spray to keep the bully from biting. Over weeks, or sometimes even months, ferrets usually learn to like or at least tolerate each other. But if yours don't, your only option is to keep them housed separately and provide separate playtimes. Otherwise, the underdog could become seriously stressed.

Chapter Three
Nipping Is a No-No

Nip it in the bud

One thing that ferret owners need to know is that ferret kits go through a nippy stage when they're about eight or nine weeks old. Why is this? In the litter, rough-and-tumble is the name of the game. Chasing, batting, swatting, darting, bounding, rolling, wrestling, and nipping are all part of playtime. It's important to realize that this is not fighting behavior . . . it's just how ferrets play. And it may not occur to your kit to stop the roughhousing just because his address and playmates have changed.

Do you have a little hooligan on your hands? You'll have to teach him to mind his manners. Don't let your pet get away with any nipping at all. Every time he nips, hold him about a foot from your face, look him straight in the eye, and say a short, sharp "NO!"

Another approach involves the use of a small ferret chew toy. Whenever your kit nips, say a firm "NO!" and give him an edible chew toy to mouth. This redirects the negative behavior (nipping) to an acceptable alternative (chewing).

You can also try to get the no-nip message across by popping your pet into his cage for a "time-out." Or, your can mimic Mama Ferret. Hold him by the scruff of the neck and give him a *little* shake, or drag him *gently* along the floor. Add a hiss or two and you'll be the perfect overbearing parent.

What about the incorrigible kit who's not getting the message? Don't despair. Instead of wringing your hands, spray them with a bitter spray (see "The carrot and the stick," page 7). Your terrible-tasting fingers will soon teach your pet that nipping is a no-no. A word of warning here. When you're spraying your hands, be careful that the spray doesn't go anywhere near your pet's face.

Treat your kit kindly when you're teaching him to mind his manners. Never point an angry finger at him and avoid using his name when he's being disciplined. In all training, your pet needs to connect his name with pleasantries.

How do you scruff a ferret? Hold him up by the loose skin at the back of his neck.

Twinkle toes

It's no secret that ferrets love to get wound up when they play. When your bundle of energy is bouncing around, ping-ponging back and forth, don't be surprised if your toes become a target—especially toes in panty hose. Toes are just too tantalizing for a ferret to ignore. But toe nipping is something *you* can't ignore. The Ferret Fandango may seem like fun when your ferret's a kit, but it won't be so cute when he's an adult.

When your kit does a nip-and-run or takes a shine to your socks, pick him up and say a firm "NO!" Then redirect his energy to another fun activity. If he has a real foot fetish, whip out the bitter spray and spritz those tootsies (yours, not his!). The bitter taste should quickly turn him off your toes. If there are any relapses, spray again.

Don't ever play footsies with your ferret. Wiggling your toes under his nose will just confuse him. He won't know when a toe attack is okay and when it's not.

Rehab hints

Are you one of the admirable owners giving an adult adoptee a second chance? Good for you! The rewards can be heartwarming. Many ferrets adjust to a new home with enthusiasm and soon become part of the family. For others, the road is a little rockier. Ferrets who have been neglected or mistreated may nip or even bite out of fear. Kindness, patience, and understanding are in order here. Your aim is to build trust, but this can be difficult with a fearful ferret. He's afraid, so he bites you; you're afraid, so you won't handle him. How do you break this cycle and begin bonding?

Find a sturdy pair of garden gloves and spray them liberally with bitter spray. Wear a long-sleeved shirt and spray the sleeves as well. Now you'll be able to hold the ferret and give him the attention he needs. Handle him frequently for short periods and follow the instructions for bonding in Chapter 2. This way, he'll begin to associate you with good things—brushing, stroking, talking gently, getting treats. Keep discipline to a minimum and reward him generously for good behavior. If he becomes truly unmanageable, time out in the cage can help him calm down.

It could take weeks for the newcomer to respond. Building trust takes time, but hang in there. After a while you'll be able to give up the gloves and just spray your hands. The final step is when trust triumphs and the bitter spray goes back on the shelf.

Chapter Four
Safe and Sound

Safety first

Your ferret is a unique pet with somewhat eccentric tastes. Run-of-the-mill catnip or milkbones are not for her, thank you! A Lysol cocktail or rubber appetizer is more up her alley. And forget that cozy spot in front of the fire. Dark, claustrophobic spaces are what attract your furry friend.

It's because ferrets eat unusual things and get into unusual places that ferret-proofing is absolutely essential. Your mission is simple—make the space safe. Crawl around on your hands and knees in every room your pet will roam and ask yourself the following questions—Can she eat it? Can she drink it? Can she open it? Can she get into it? Can she get stuck in it? Can she escape from it?

Take the house tour in this chapter. You'll learn to look at your home from a ferret's point of view and size up potential hazards. You'll also get practical ferret-proofing solutions. Read through every section in this chapter and zero in on whatever applies to your place.

A clean sweep in the kitchen

Take one ferret, pop her into the average kitchen, look the other way, and you'll have a recipe for disaster. Wherever she turns, there's temptation. Soap, dishwashing detergent, cleansers, plant sprays—all these forbidden fruits will draw her like a magnet. That's no big problem, you might think—just stow the stuff in the cupboards. Wrong! You haven't seen anything until you've seen ferret paws pry open a door or a drawer. An easy way to take care of this problem is to store everything in seal-tight containers. Another option is to install baby locks. But beware. Not all childproof locks are ferret-proof. With some baby locks, you have to open the drawer or door a little bit to disengage the locking mechanism. But if your ferret can open a drawer or cupboard even a little bit, she can probably weasel her way right in, because ferrets can crawl into very small spaces. So what kind of locks should you look for? Magnetic locks used for baby-

Make your home safe for your tireless explorer.

proofing are ideal. They will stymie even the most determined ferret. Just don't misplace the magnetic key . . . or neither one of you will get into the cupboards!

Rubber is *the* ferret favorite, so keep sink mats, sink stoppers, silicone bakeware, and rubber gloves out of reach. Check also for bumpers on cabinet or refrigerator doors. Anything made of sponge also has a fatal attraction for your ferret. Keep all sponges in closed margarine tubs and store mops with their heads up, not down at ferret level.

Does your little scamp like rifling through the garbage? A pedal bin or step-on trash can will prevent ferret foraging. Does your nosy kit try getting into the oven storage drawer? Install an oven or appliance lock, the kind used for baby-proofing, or tape the drawer shut. Also tape the refrigerator kickplate so she can't get at the motor, coils, and insulation.

Your ferret's svelte and sinuous body (the kind you've always dreamed of) allows her to slink behind, between, and beneath the fridge, the dishwasher, and the cupboard kickboards. To keep her out of harm's way, arm yourself with sturdy cardboard and duct tape. Block off any spaces larger than one inch across by cutting cardboard to fit and anchoring it with tape. For larger spaces, fold the cardboard and wedge it into place. Ferret-proofing around a kitchen stove or oven is not quite so simple. Fire code regulations may require a space between an oven and the adjacent cabinet. Your best plan is to contact your local by-law officer or fire department and ask for advice.

Use cord protectors to prevent your pet from chewing on electrical wires.

A guest in the living room?

Grab a cup of coffee, head for the living room, and have a good look around. Ask yourself whether you want your ferret in here. If not, French doors, folding doors, or louvered doors could be the answer. Do you need a cheaper and less permanent solution? On the left inside door frame, make a track by attaching two thin strips of wood a half-inch apart. Do the same on the right side. Stain or paint the tracks to match the woodwork, then slot in a piece of Plexiglas. Voila! Limited admission.

But, if your pet's going to be welcome, take a few precautions *before* letting her loose. Move those knick-knacks off the tables before she does and keep drinks out of reach. If your kit shows an interest in a lamp cord, smear it with a nontoxic, bitter cream or gel—the kind used to stop pets from chewing. Creams and gels don't drip, and they last longer than sprays. Another option is to enclose the cord in a cord protector, the type specially designed to deter pets. This plastic tubing has a bitter scent and a bitter taste, and is not easy to chew through.

Watch out, too, for hot-water radiators. Little heads can get stuck in little places. To protect your ferret, install radiator covers. Look for the ones that fit snug to the floor, because a cover won't do any good if your ferret can crawl under it. If you already have radiator covers that are raised up on legs, you'll need to attach wire screening around the bottoms to keep your pet out.

Before you go flopping on the sofa to catch forty winks, take a quick look under the cushions. A ferret couch potato could be hogging the spot already. Speaking of the sofa, your ferret might pry back the gauzy material underneath so she can crawl inside. What a great hidey hole for snoozing or caching loot! If your pet tries this trick, staple the material back to the frame and dab it with a bitter cream or gel. If she's persistent, you may have to resort to stapling small-holed chicken wire across the underside. Don't fret. No one but your ferret will see it anyway! And it's much better than having a stowaway in your sofa.

An enterprising ferret, looking for adventure, might pull out a heating vent and crawl into the duct work. Warning! Warning! She could get lost or hurt. Spare yourself the hassle; check your vent covers. Some have tabs on the sides that can be pried out with a screwdriver to ensure a tighter fit. Others will have to be screwed to the floor.

Windows and doors can sometimes present problems when you have a ferret. For example, any foam or rubber weather stripping can be quite appetizing for a fuzzy. Here's another job for a bitter spray, gel, or cream. Apply it to any weather stripping within ferret reach. Some ferrets are real escape artists. If they can reach a window or a screen door, they'll rip out the screen, hop outside, and take a hike. Fortunately, you can replace your current window or door screening with tough pet-proof screening; a ferret can't claw through this. Another idea to keep your pet away from window screens is to position a narrow electrostatic pet mat on the window ledge and tape it down with wide tape, such as masking, packing, or duct tape. Your ferret will soon get the message to stay away from the windowsill. See Chapter 17 for the scoop on electrostatic pet mats.

Ferrets can squeeze into small spaces—be sure to block off any trouble spots.

One of the easiest ways to lose a ferret is for someone to open a door to the outside and give the furball a great chance to sneak off. (That's one good reason to keep a bell on her collar!) So when you're coming and going, make sure your ferret's not shooting out the door unnoticed. And, be absolutely certain that everyone in the family closes *every* door to the outside, *every* time, or Pippi will go AWOL.

Focus on the family room

Family room frolics can be fast and furious with a ferret around. But before the fun begins, ferret-proof, ferret-proof, ferret-proof.

At the top of the list is the reclining chair. Ferrets like to climb inside these chairs and can get stuck or crushed in the mechanism. Do you know where Pippi's sleeping when you put your feet up for a rest? Because these chairs are a major cause of injury to ferrets, most books recommend getting rid of them. But if Mom won't part with her favorite lounger, a cheap and easy solution is to disable the chair by doctoring the footrest and the reclining back.

First, disable the footrest. If there's a side lever, remove it. Where there's a push button, upend the chair and disconnect the cable that operates the footrest. When all else fails, take strong rope or clothesline and tie the metal footrest supports to an immovable part of the chair frame.

Next, inactivate the reclining back. Upend the chair and look for the two large wing nuts that control the reclining mechanism. Tighten these as much as possible. For chairs with sliding tracks, cut two wooden dowels or slats and insert one in each track.

Last, stuff any openings around the bottom of the now non-recliner with cardboard taped into place or with rolled chicken wire because a ferret can get stuck even in a disabled mechanism.

A rocking recliner is a bigger safety headache yet. Rockers crush ferrets. So after you've fixed the footrest and the back, you must stop the rocking motion. Shove a wooden wedge under the back and

Ferrets like to nap in recliners and sofa beds. Ferret-proof your furniture to avoid accidents.

front of each rocker and secure it with duct tape. Regular rocking chairs should be relocated to a ferret-free zone.

If you have an oddball chair that's in a class of its own or you don't trust your fix-it skills, trot on down to your friendly furniture store and ask the service person for advice. Test any adjustments you make to ensure that you no longer have a recliner or a rocking recliner. Your ferret's worth the sacrifice!

With sofa beds, not only is the mechanism a concern, but Pippi can also crawl into the folded mattress and get stuck, sat on, or smothered. What's the solution? Keep her out by blocking off the bottom. Open up the bed and line the inside edges of the sofa frame with lengths of scrap 2×4-inch wood, cut or pieced to fit. In some spots where wood won't fit, cardboard and duct tape will.

Do you like to unwind by watching TV after a long day? Then make sure to keep an eye on your ferret as well as on your favorite show. Why? Most ferrets love remote controls, and will take every opportunity to run off with them. Not only could they end up in Pippi's stockpile, but even worse, she could chew off the rubber buttons and get an intestinal blockage.

For the most part, televisions themselves are not a problem where ferrets are concerned. But small, flat-screen TVs are another matter because ferrets can knock them over. To avoid accidents, either mount the TV on a wall, or purchase the television straps used to prevent TVs from toppling in an earthquake.

Take time to ferret-proof . . . it's not good for your pet to spend too much time in her cage.

Are you a television video-game junkie? You'll need to be vigilant about keeping your equipment out of ferret reach, because there's absolutely no way you can make this gaming stuff ferret safe. Much of the equipment has rubber or silicone components. Think of the wireless controllers with their rubberized buttons and knobs, the nonslip silicone covers for the controllers, and the remote accessories like drums, guitars, balance boards, and steering wheels. These are all potential hazards for ferrets, so keep your pet out of the room while games are in progress, and make sure everything is carefully locked away when game time is over.

Anyone who has a surround-sound and/or stereo system will need to watch out for ferret attacks on the speakers. Speakers are like magnets for ferrets because of the foam that's used in their construction. You can't see the foam, but your pet can certainly smell it. Some ferrets can pop off the front panels of speakers in no time flat, or scratch through the fabric covering of the panels, to wreak havoc on those woofers and tweeters. Take steps to protect your investment. Small speakers can be put up on shelves, hung on a wall, or placed on pedestals, but large floor speakers are more difficult to keep out of ferret reach. One option would be to keep your music critic out of the room. Or, you could slide an electrostatic pet mat under the front of each speaker and secure the mat to the floor with one-inch-wide tape to prevent your ferret from crawling underneath. See Chapter 17 for information about electrostatic pet mats.

Does your stereo or surround-sound system include a subwoofer? This can be a real headache if you have a ferret. Not only can ferrets pry off the front panel to get at the foam, but they can also get inside some subwoofers via tubes in the back, front, or sides. Another problem with a subwoofer is that it's designed to go on the floor, just where it's easiest for a ferret to get at it. What's the answer? If it's the tubes that are a problem, you could block them off by inserting circles of wire screening (bent like jar lids) into the openings and anchoring them in place with duct tape. If the front panel is a target, you could move the subwoofer off the floor, out of ferret reach, but this will compromise the sound of your CDs and DVDs. Another possibility is to make a wire "cage" for the subwoofer. It won't look the best, but it will keep your fuzzy's paws off both the front and the back of the equipment. If you're in the market for a new subwoofer, there are now brands on the market that are rodent proof—no fabric fronts and no accessible tubes. Do an Internet search for *subwoofer rodent proof*.

Rec room review

Anyone for ping-pong? Your ferret will be happy to retrieve the balls. She'll also be happy to nibble the rubber off your ping-pong paddles. So watch where you set them down. If pool is your pastime, keep an eye on your cue. Your ferret will have her eye on the rubber tip. Be alert and check any games for small pieces of rubber or foam that could cause internal blockage if swallowed.

Is the rec room the hobby center of the house? Wine makers, store plastic tubing and corks well out of reach. Crafters, safeguard your supplies. Model enthusiasts, keep your kits out of your kits. Artists, guard those gum erasers. Get the picture?

If you have retired an elderly sofa or chair to the rec room, inspect all seams for leaks. Some ferrets eat shredded foam. You can repair a torn seam with heavy quilting thread and a curved upholstery needle, or try using duct tape. It sticks to almost anything. If the underside of the furniture has seen better days, use the chicken wire solution (see page 21) or take off the furniture's legs.

Overhauling the office

Whether you have a fully equipped home office or make do with a desk in the corner, you'll have your furry friend nosing around. No, she's not after your official secrets. What she really wants are those ferret favorites—rubber bands, erasers, and stick tack. Other tasty tidbits are calculator buttons and plastic sleeves for computer disks. And have you ever noticed those little protective pads under lamps, desk organizers, telephones, and so on? These cork or rubber bumpers are bad news for tiny tummies, and they turn up on many more items than you might realize.

It's a rare office that doesn't have a computer, and most ferret owners don't realize what a field day a ferret can have around a computer and its various add-ons. For example, some monitors have silicone adjustment buttons, and some keyboards are now made entirely of silicone. The sides of many computer mouses have silicone panels, and mouse pads are often made of foam or Neoprene. Some portable hard drives have a rubberized outer coating, and wireless routers often have rubberized antennas.

When using your laptop, keep a watchful eye on your fuzzy.

Flash drives, memory sticks, and their cases often end up in ferret stockpiles. Although many of the sticks are made of plastic or metal, some of them now have a soft-touch rubberized coating, and the cases are frequently made of Neoprene. It won't be cute if your fuzzy chews on one of these and swallows some synthetic rubber. If you have a laptop, be sure to keep any cords, Neoprene sleeves, and foam-padded carry bags well away from your furball. Ditto for microphones, headphones, and webcams. And don't forget to check the buttons on your copier/fax/scanner—many are rubberized and could be chewed off.

While you're getting into your hard drive, your pet could be getting into the file cabinet (keep it closed) and the wastebasket (get one with a lid) and up into the desk drawers from behind (use cardboard and duct tape to close any openings). Ferrets also like to reprogram the answering machine. So if you've missed any messages, check with your ferret!

Bed and bath

When it comes to the bedroom, don't be caught napping, or you could open your sock drawer and find more than you bargained for! Better remove ferret-unfriendly items from drawers, or ferret-proof dressers with cardboard and duct tape.

Does your ferret treat your box springs as a safety deposit box? By tearing away a small corner of the gauze covering, she can get inside and cache her valuables—or yours. You can put a stop to this the same way you took care of the sofa in the living room.

A child's bedroom should be out of bounds. A million and one things in it are ferret unfriendly. Can you guarantee that toy car wheels, super balls, balloons, ear plugs, play clay, foam, flip-flops, and so on are always out of reach?

Before your buddy makes whoopee in the bathroom, stash all cotton balls and swabs, sponges, and feminine hygiene products. Lock up the Lysol and keep the soap out of sight. After your Saturday morning cleaning blitz, don't leave the toilet brush lying around; your ferret will lap up the leftover cleanser. Put away the brush holder, too. Drippings that pool in the bottom can be tempting. Pull the plug after your bath—ferrets can climb into the tub. And watch your step! Towels, clothes, and throw rugs on the floor could be concealing a kit.

Don't forget to plug any openings around the plumbing pipes with stainless steel pot scrubbers (not the steel wool variety), chicken wire, Polyfilla, or cardboard and duct tape. You don't want your ferret wandering around in your walls or paying unscheduled visits to the next apartment. When plugging up holes around plumbing pipes, you might be tempted to use spray insulating foam. But don't. Although this stuff does a good job of filling up holes, your ferret's liable to eat it.

Down to the basement

If you let your ferret run about in the cellar, you could be singing the basement blues. Ferrets like to hole up in warm, dark spots. If your little Pippi crawls inside the furnace or under the hot-water tank, singed whiskers could be the least of her problems. She could get scorched or badly burned. To prevent accidents, the whole furnace area should be off limits.

Keep the dehumidifier ferret free with . . .

Is your basement on the damp side with a dehumidifier as part of the decor? A resourceful ferret can pull out the water container and help herself to a drink—and another and another and another, until she gets sick. Thwart her efforts with tape or Velcro.

Do you keep tripping over sports equipment drying in the basement? When checking your gear for mildew, check it also for foam, rubber, or sponge. Ferrets will tackle tennis shoe insoles, rubber squash balls, soccer shin guards, baseball shoe cleats, and the padding in football and hockey gear. You could stuff the equipment into a sports bag, but be aware that unzipping zippers is an uncanny ferret talent.

The laundry room

It's probably safer to keep your ferret out of the laundry room altogether. It's not just the detergent, fabric softener, stain removers, and bleach she can get at. She might sneak under the washer and nibble the drive belts, chew through the dryer vent and crawl outside, or get

. . . Velcro or tape.

Curious kits looking for mischief—what better reason to ferret-proof?

tossed into the wash when snoozing in the dirty clothes.

If the laundry room can't be closed off, ferret-proof it. Board up any openings. Replace flexible vinyl or aluminum/polyester dryer venting with either rigid aluminum or flexible compressed aluminum venting, and clamp, tape, or bolt it securely in place. And always sift through the laundry carefully—ferrets are strictly "hand wash and towel dry."

Safety on the stairway

When you're racing up or down stairs, yield to fast-moving ferrets overtaking from behind or changing lanes in front. Accidents can happen. A ferret darts back and forth so quickly, it's easy for her to be trampled underfoot. The best way to avoid serious injury is to let her go ahead or carry her.

All around the house

There are some everyday items that family members use all around the house and move frequently from room to room. MP3 players are a good example. How many people in your house have one, and where are they right now? The fact is, lots of people use MP3 players and tend to leave them lying here, there, and everywhere. Yet these players and all the accessories are hugely tempting to a ferret.

Depending on the brand, MP3 players may have rubberized dials or buttons that can be easily chewed off. Many of the accessories such as docking platforms, USB cords, headphones, ear buds, mini–speaker systems, and armbands have rubberized components. And what about those Neoprene, synthetic leather, and silicone covers for MP3 players . . . the ones that come in all those trendy colors? You might find a big stockpile of these in your pet's favorite hiding place. Unfortunately, they can be shredded pretty easily and ingested by your ferret.

Car keys are something else that people tend to leave lying around the house. Are you one of those people who are always looking for your car keys, remote starters, remote openers, and so forth? It's very possible that your ferret will find your key chain before you do . . . and hide it. If you can't find your chain and there's a transponder key on it, expect sticker shock when you have the lost key replaced at the dealership. To avoid these problems, keep your keys in one place, well out of ferret reach.

How many cell phones are scattered around your house? You shouldn't leave these lying around, because they're just the right size for ferrets to drag off to who-knows-where. Although the plastic or metal models might not be so tempting to furballs, others have silicone buttons or a nonslip, rubberized coating that ferrets can't resist. Hands-free headsets, portable cordless phones, and charger cords are also extremely attractive to ferrets—it's the foam and rubber they go for.

When's the last time you laid eyes on your digital camera? If you haven't seen it lately, could your furball be downloading the photos? You need to keep cameras and camcorders—along with their batteries, carry bags, cords, and lenses—in a safe place, well out of ferret reach.

All done!

Now that you're completely overwhelmed by what you've just read, take heart. Every house and ferret is different. There's not much chance that everything mentioned in this chapter will apply to your situation. Ferret-proofing may seem like work, but the suggested solutions don't involve a lot of time or money. And after all, isn't it worth a little effort to keep your ferret safe and sound?

Chapter Five

Exploring the Environment

Curious critters

To say that your ferret is inquisitive is an understatement. When it comes to curiosity, a ferret beats a cat hands down. He's the Sherlock Holmes of the animal kingdom, a true detective who'll peer, pry, and probe into every hole and corner. How do you think the term *ferret out* came about?

You don't have to train your ferret to investigate his environment. Exploration is basic to his nature. He'll do it automatically and enthusiastically. But you will have a job to do. You'll need to direct and supervise his activities and, of course, to ferret-proof each room before he has access to it. (You did read Chapter 4, didn't you?)

Decisions, decisions

Before you set your super sleuth loose, you'll have to give some thought to his field of operation. Some ferrets are kept mainly in their cages and let out for two or three lengthy exercise periods per day. Others are allowed out of their cages all the time. Most fall somewhere in between. Some ferrets have one room designated as an exercise and play area, whereas others have full run of the house or apartment. Again, most fall somewhere in between. What's the best way to go for you and your pet? How much freedom and how much territory will he be allowed?

To help you decide, here's a list of questions to ask yourself. How much time do you have to spend supervising your ferret's antics? How big is your house or apartment? What is the layout of your living space? How easy is it to keep your ferret out of certain rooms? How determined is your pet? How rambunctious is he? How house-friendly is he? How tolerant are you? How many litter boxes are you willing to clean? And, most important, can you guarantee his safety?

There are no right or wrong answers. Every household is different.

Is it playtime yet?

Every ferret is different. What you decide will be based on your individual circumstances. And your decision needn't be written in stone. You may want to re-evaluate when you and your ferret know each other better. Keep in mind, though, that a ferret is a companion pet, not a cage animal.

No matter how much freedom you allow your pet, he should always be in his cage when you are sleeping or out of the house. Otherwise, his safety will be seriously compromised. Remember the old saying, "Curiosity killed the cat"? Well, your ferret doesn't have nine lives like a cat.

Limiting turf

So how do you get off to a good start when introducing Sherlock to his new surroundings? "Elementary, my dear Watson!" Limit his turf. A small area is less overwhelming and gives him a chance to explore safely. It gives you more control and the opportunity to see what he can get into. This is when you find out if you paid enough attention to Chapter 4.

If your ferret is to be confined to a one-room headquarters, his turf is limited automatically. If he'll eventually roam your whole house, you need to restrict his investigations to one room at first. Pick a small room or block off part of a large one.

If this is a place where you plan to keep a litter box, be sure to introduce him to it right away. Even if he just used the pan in his cage, he needs to know where this one is. If this is not an area where you plan to have a litter box, put him back in his cage every twenty to thirty minutes for a potty break.

The investigator

Wait until your ferret has wakened and used the litter box in his cage before his first foray. Speaking softly, pick him up gently and cuddle him. Then, take him over to the space you've designated as the first exploration site. Sit down (at floor level if possible), let him loose, and watch carefully.

Once he gets a whiff of freedom, Sherlock will start to case the joint—investigating cupboards, peering under furniture, seeking out adventure. He'll sniff each and every square inch, usually following the perimeter of the area first. Every nook and cranny will get the once over, even the twice or thrice over! You might want to put a few toys in the area, but he probably won't be interested until he's finished exploring this uncharted territory. In fact, don't try to distract him from his mission. Let him explore to his heart's content. Remember that the whole idea of this exercise is to get your pet accustomed to his new environment. You might want to play, but he will want to snoop.

Expanding horizons

For a few days or longer, stick to the same old scene and the same old routine. Let Sherlock get completely comfortable with the territory before increasing his play area. Then gradually, over weeks, expand his range one room at a time. In each new room, give your little gumshoe a chance to check out the joint under your watchful eye. You may decide that some places in the house can't be adequately ferret-proofed and need to be off limits for your nosy critter. And that's okay.

On guard

As a responsible ferret owner, you always have to keep an eye open for calamities waiting to happen. You never know when someone could leave an outside door open or drop a rubber band or forget to close a cupboard. For you, the case is never closed. Like the faithful Watson, you've got to be Sherlock's right-hand man, watching out for his well-being.

Chapter Six

Poop Goes the Weasel

Litter training—fact or fiction?

Is your little furball a potty pro, semi-pro, veteran, or rookie? Will the accidents stop this year, next year, sometime, never? What *are* the facts about litter training ferrets? The good news is that, yes, your ferret can be trained to use a litter pan. The not so good news is that most will have the occasional accident. People tend to judge litter pan success by cat standards. However, you have a ferret for a pet, not a cat. And ferret standards aren't always as accurate. A lot depends upon the individual ferret, how much time she spends in her cage, how much of the house or apartment she roams, how big the rooms are, and how many litter pans you provide. Some ferrets will use the box 100 percent of the time. A rare ferret will make only sporadic visits. But, fortunately, most can be trained to use the box most of the time.

Litter box lowdown

To increase the odds of success, make sure that the bathroom facilities are adequate. Pay attention to the type of litter pan you buy. Ferrets back up into a corner and lift their tails before relieving themselves. If you pick a box with low sides, the mess will just drop over the side and onto the floor. What you need is a

Pick a litter pan with high sides and a low entry.

Newspaper keeps the floor clean under a litter box.

pan with high sides for backups, and a low entranceway for short legs. Most litter boxes and pans made specifically for ferrets fit the bill, though some ferrets won't use triangular boxes. Your best plan is to buy the biggest square or rectangular boxes you can find, because ferrets like to get their whole bodies into the box when they do their business. Some cat pans with low entryways might also be suitable. Because ferrets like privacy on the job, boxes with hoods are a good choice as long as the doorway is ferret accessible. A ferret that can't get into her box easily will take the easy way out and plop elsewhere.

Ferrets won't go far to find a litter box, so if your pet is allowed into several rooms, she'll need several boxes. Will this be a strain on your budget? Then why not make your own litter boxes? Buy plastic storage containers or dishpans approximately 16 inches long × 10 inches wide × 7 inches high (or larger). Provide entranceways by cutting out a 6 × 6-inch section from one of the 10 inch sides of each box. Don't cut the hole too close to the bottom of the box, or you'll end up having more litter out of the boxes than in! Use a handheld rotary tool or a hacksaw to make the cuts, and be sure to wear protective eyewear when doing the job. Then sand the cut edges to give a smooth finish.

Ferrets are prolific poopers, so scoop out the waste once or twice daily. Wash the box weekly with plain soap and water or a nontoxic pet-odor neutralizer. Not too thrilled about cleaning litter boxes? You can avoid this chore by buying disposable litter boxes made from recycled paper. As an added plus, they're biodegradable.

To keep the area around litter boxes clean, place plastic carpet runner under each box and tape it to the floor. Newspaper is acceptable too, if your ferret doesn't shred it or eat it.

Pick of the litter

No one litter is perfect for every ferret. There are pros and cons with each type, so weigh the differences and make the choice that's best for you and your pet. Your first consideration should be to find something that agrees with your ferret. Then consider your pocketbook, your

Inexpensive plastic storage boxes . . .

. . . make good homemade litter boxes.

environmental commitment, and your clean-up tolerance.

Regular clay and clumping clay cat litters used to be popular choices for ferret litter, but there are problems associated with them. To start with, the clay can cause skin and fur dryness. Also, a ferret tunneling through clay litter can develop eye irritations or respiratory problems from the silica dust in the litter. Sometimes clay particles can stick to ferret paws and rectums, and can be ingested if your pet licks herself. And, if the particles stick to the genital area, urinary tract infections can develop.

Many experienced ferret owners now recommend pelleted paper litter. This litter is made of recycled paper, so it's a good environmental choice. It doesn't track through the house, it's absorbent, and odor control is good. The pellets are virtually dust-free when poured out of the bag, but they become dusty as they break down, and should be replaced regularly. Watch that your pet doesn't mistake the pellets for dinner. If she does, switch to a different type of litter.

Wood pellets are another popular choice for the litter box. Like paper pellets, they have excellent absorbency and odor control. Also, like paper pellets, they become dusty as they break down. You have two choices here. You can either buy hardwood woodstove pellets, which come in bulk and are cheap. Or, you can buy the packaged wood pellets that are marketed as pet litter. These come in two types—the hardwood litter (look for aspen wood), and the heat-treated softwood (look for kiln-dried pine). When buying wood litter, stay away from shavings and from pellets made from cedar or untreated pine. These products contain phenols that can cause respiratory and liver problems in small animals.

There are some excellent grain-based litters available. Some are corn-based, some are wheat-based, some are oat-based, and some are made from wheat straw. Some of these are flushable and some are clumping. You might have to try a few to find one that you and your ferret both like.

Whatever litter you choose, don't change from week to week with the sales. Your ferret might boycott her box if it contains something new. If you must change types, start by putting the new litter into the box and cover it with a layer of the old. Gradually increase the new and decrease the old until you've changed over completely. When switching litters, always keep a close eye on your ferret. If she starts eating or caching the new stuff, get rid of it.

Alternatives to litter boxes and litter

If the idea of daily litter scooping and weekly box cleaning doesn't rank high on your list of exciting activities, or if your ferret takes to playing or sleeping in her litter or eating it, then you might want to give pet potty pads a try. Some of these are made specifically for ferrets. They look a bit like traditional ferret litter pans, fitting neatly into a corner and extending a few inches up the wall. If you can't find them at your local pet store, do an Internet search for *ferret potty pads*. Other potty pads are flat mats that fit into awkward spaces between or behind furniture. You can buy made-for-ferret flat pads, or use puppy pads instead. All of these products are highly absorbent and disposable.

Another cheap and easy idea is to place a piece of plastic carpet runner in the corner, or anywhere else your ferret has decided to do her business. Tape it securely to the floor and partway up the wall; then lay newspaper on top of it. Toss out the soiled paper regularly, and wipe the plastic clean.

Cage training

When nature calls, ferrets back into a corner, lift their tails, and answer. Take advantage of this habit and place the litter box in a corner of the cage, ready to catch the droppings. The problem is that the potty pan won't stay in the corner long if your pet has her way. Many ferrets keep busy, busy, busy arranging and rearranging the contents of their cages. The litter box is a prime target, and your industrious scene shifter will pull, push, drag, and tip even the best of boxes. The best solution to this problem is to buy a lock-on litter box that attaches to the cage wires. Or, you can buy a regular litter box and attach it to the cage with universal cage clips (found in pet stores or on the Internet). You could also attach it to the cage just like the dishes on page 5. Or, you could make holes in the box with a hot nail and wire it to the cage. Another option is to go on the Internet and search for a *ferret custom litter box*. These litter boxes fit across the whole of one cage side, and can be made to fit any size of cage. Because the pan is an exact fit, your fuzzy can't move it around.

Now it's time to get down to business. You'll have a head start on litter training if your kit has come from a breeder or shop where a litter pan has been available to her from day one. She'll already have the right idea about that box in the corner. But, if you're starting from scratch, here's a handy hint. A ferret uses the litter pan within minutes of waking. So catch her after a snooze, when she's starting her backward wiggle, and deposit her in the box. She'll soon learn that's where she's supposed to go. If she doesn't catch on, or plays and sleeps in the litter, give the box that lived-in look. Put in some droppings along with a urine-soaked paper towel and sprinkle some litter on top. Then pop her into the pan for a good sniff around. When she uses the box, bring out the treats! Each successful hit deserves a generous reward. She needs to get the message that going in the box is a good thing.

What's this? Your pet has found a different corner of the cage with more ferret appeal? It's much easier to place the box in her chosen corner than to fight about it. Ferrets can be stubborn and she'll always win. If you're still not having any luck, try partitioning off part of the cage so that she's left with only enough room for food, bedding, and box. She's not likely to soil her eating or sleeping area, so she won't have much option but to use the box. Try to catch her in the act and reward her. When she's visiting the box regularly, give her back her space.

When your ferret's ready to go, she'll back up into a corner with tail raised.

House training

For most owners, cage training runs smoothly. But your kit won't always be confined to her cage so you'll have to work on litter training around the house at the same time. The job is not as easy when she's outside the cage running around, exploring, and having fun. With so many exciting distractions, her attention just won't be focused on the litter box.

You might think a pan in the cage is all that's needed. However, once your investigator is out and about,

"Sorry. I missed the box!"

she won't be too eager to trot back into her cage for a bathroom break. After all, the door to freedom could slam shut behind her. So it makes sense to have a box in her play area as well as a box in her cage.

Start your ferret's house training in the room where she's starting to explore the environment. Put a litter box in a convenient corner, prime it with poop, set her inside, and give her a treat. Whenever she makes a repeat visit, praise her warmly and repeat the reward. If, however, you find her backing into another corner with tail up high, this is your signal to hightail her into the pan. You might have to hold her there gently for a few seconds until she performs. Got a ferret with attitude who insists on leaping out? Keep your eye on her until she backs up again, then whisk her into the box as often as necessary until the mission is accomplished. Or, if she's making repeated attempts in a different spot, take the hint—that's where she wants her bathroom, so move the box. Then for every successful visit, dish out a treat—a little bribery works miracles. Try to slip her the reward right after she's done her business and before she leaves the box. She needs all the encouragement she can get to hit the jackpot every time.

So far, so good. When there's only one room to worry about, most ferrets get the hang of things pretty quickly. The real challenge comes when your ferret starts to explore more of the house. There are corners galore! And, for reasons known only to ferrets, when they make the rounds of several rooms, they won't always bother going far to find a box. So, to avoid accidents, you'll need to place at least one litter box, if not more, in every room your pet is allowed into.

Accidents will happen

Even the best-trained ferret can have accidents. If you catch the culprit in the act, say a loud, firm "NO!" and add a loud handclap before carting her off to the nearest box. Never rub her nose in the mess and don't spank her—she won't understand. When you find her calling card in the corner, but she's fled the scene of the accident, discipline after the fact won't do a bit of good.

Is your ferret a repeat offender in a particular spot? Don't bother with spray repellents; they seldom work. A better solution is to scatter some dry food over the area. Ferrets will rarely go potty where there's food. Does your pet gobble down the food and poop in the spot anyway? It's not worth the aggravation to argue over it. Why not go with the flow and put another litter box there?

Your ferret might be absolutely wonderful about her litter box stops for weeks on end, and then, bingo!, little piles will appear here, there, and everywhere but in the box. What gives? A little ferret nose just might be out of joint. Have you been gone a lot lately? Have other pets been over to play? This backsliding is a ferret's way of saying, "I'll show you a thing or two—or three or four!" Don't take it personally. Give her a few extra cuddles, and she'll be back to normal in no time. Or she may be backsliding because she's miffed about the state of her box. Some ferrets prefer a scrupulously clean pan; others favor a slightly used one. If your ferret ignores her facilities, perhaps her housekeeping standards are different from yours. In cases where litter habits go totally out of whack or stools are abnormal, it's important to schedule a visit to the veterinarian.

When accidents do happen, it's important to clean up thoroughly, because ferrets have a powerful sense of smell and will often reuse an area where they can smell urine or feces. Fortunately, accidents are not hard to clean up. Just pick up poops with a tissue, and blot urine with paper towels. Then wash the area well with a vinegar solution, rinse it with plain water, and spray with a pet urine neutralizer.

If you can't handle the occasional accident, or if you have acquired a ferret whose habits aren't the best, perhaps you need to train yourself rather than your ferret. Don't let her out of the cage until she's used the pan, and you'll be one step ahead. When she's out romping around, watch for that backup signal and rush her to the nearest box. And when she falls asleep, always put her back in the cage so that she'll be right beside the litter pan when she wakes up. If you are still having trouble, confining her activities to one room will help with damage control.

Repetition and reward

It helps to keep in mind that kits are babies, and miracles don't happen overnight. For both kits and older adoptees, patience and understanding are important. Don't yell, scream, or get frustrated. Do reward, reward, reward. Remember that most ferrets can be taught to use the litter box most of the time. So hang in there and, before you know it, your ferret will be minding her pees and poos.

Chapter Seven

Coming When Called

"I'm a calling youuuu . . ."

Many ferret owners don't realize that their pet can be taught to come when called by name. This is not just a trick. It's a useful skill that may come in handy if your ferret ever escapes or gets into the heating ducts by mistake (surely his mistake and not yours!).

Your kit will never respond to his name like a dog will. If you have a mental image of your ferret bounding up to you, sitting back on his haunches, thumping his tail on the floor, and waiting for a pat on the head, then you're barking up the wrong tree. Your furry friend won't snap to it for praise alone: It's a tasty tidbit that will bring him running. "No goodie, forget it!" is the ferret motto.

Choosing a reward

Treats serve a dual purpose. They're an enticement to get your ferret to do something in the first place and they're used as a reward during training *every time* he successfully does what you want.

You must have a food reward that your ferret will absolutely love—beg for—die for. Finding the perfect treat, however, may not be so simple. Some ferrets can be finicky eaters. It may take a while to find that special treat, a wholesome one he'll be crazy about.

A liquid skin and coat supplement (see pages 7–8) is your bet for starters. Not only do most ferrets like these supplements, they're also good for them. The maximum daily dosage varies from brand to brand, so it's up to you to read the label carefully and figure out how much you can safely give your pet per day. Whatever the recommended amount is, don't give it to your furball all at once. What you want to do is divide the daily allowance into lots of little rewards. Are you finding that the maximum daily dosage won't provide enough rewards? Not a problem. Just mix the supplement with an equal amount of olive oil or canola oil to make it stretch further.

Another great product for rewards is a made-for-ferrets vitamin supplement that comes in paste form. Again, make sure to follow the dosage instructions carefully, because ferrets absolutely adore this stuff, and would eat the whole tube if you let them.

The different brands of supplements have different tastes. If your ferret doesn't go nuts over one, try giving him another. You'll soon find something that rates the ferret seal of approval. And when you do, make sure to keep the bottle or tube well out of ferret reach. Otherwise your fuzzy thief might steal and stash a tube, and gorge on the goodies, tube and all.

An unusual but effective reward is your ferret's fur ball medicine. You do use this as a preventive measure, don't you? Most ferrets love the stuff. Fur ball prevention medicine is usually given three times per week. Check with your veterinarian for the recommended dosage. However, make your pet work hard for this reward because, to be effective against hair balls, it needs to be gulped down at one sitting, not divided into dabs. And remember that you can use this only on the days your ferret is due to have it.

"Do I smell a treat?"

Family favorites for ferrets?

Should you feed your ferret any of your favorite food? Does table food make a good treat? Cooked boneless chicken, beef, lamb, or fish can be given to your ferret without hazard to his health, because cooked meat is protein, and protein should make up the major part of your pet's diet. However, avoid lunch meats or processed meats that contain nitrates or excess sodium. Other good protein treats include hard-boiled or scrambled eggs and pure-meat baby food (avoid the kind with added vegetables or pasta). You could also try freeze-dried, 100 percent natural, meat treats for pets.

Some owners like to give their ferrets tiny bits of fruits and vegetables like raw green pepper or cucumber, cooked carrots or broccoli, mashed bananas, unsweetened applesauce, or minute morsels of raisins, strawberries, watermelon, and blueberries. The problem is that these healthy-for-people foods contain carbohydrates and sugars, which a ferret's digestive system is not designed to process. Dairy foods are something else that a ferret can't process. So don't give your pet any milk, cheese, pudding, yogurt, or ice cream.

The same goes for junk food such as red licorice (which most ferrets love), candies, fruit-flavored or sugar-coated cereals, cake and icing, doughnuts, cookies, marshmallows, chips, and popcorn. It's tempting to offer these tasty foods because, just like you, your kit will love the very things he shouldn't have. But, for your ferret, it's not just a matter of keeping slim and trim. It's a matter of keeping healthy and free from intestinal problems.

The D-I-Y target stick

After you hit upon the gourmet treat that has your ferret drooling and licking his lips, you can start teaching him to love the sound of your voice calling his name. The first step is to make a target stick. What? You've never heard of such a thing? Well, now's your opportunity to learn all about a useful and inexpensive training tool used by the pros.

It's really simple to make. Even those who hightail it fast at the very mention of do-it-yourself projects can make one of these in a matter of minutes. You need only three items—a piece of wooden dowel or stick approximately three feet long, a plastic spoon (the kind used on picnics), and some masking or duct tape. Tape the spoon onto one end of the stick so that the spoon becomes an extension of the stick. Picture the finished product as a spoon with a long handle—a very long handle.

Now, with treat ready and stick in hand, find your ferret and off you go. Oh, one more thing—be sure you've picked out a name for your pet.

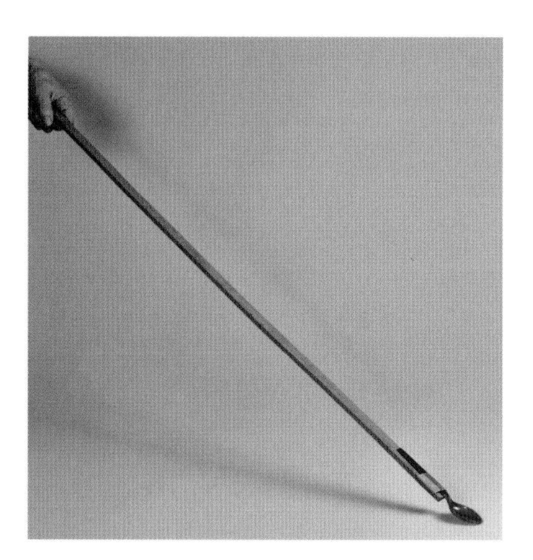

It takes just a few minutes to make this handy training aid—the target stick.

It takes two to tango

Training your ferret to come when called is much easier if two people work together. Both people should sit on the floor about two feet apart. Person A holds the ferret, and Person B holds the target stick. Place a few drops of skin and coat supplement on the spoon. Person B holds the spoon right under the student's nose and gives the command,

"Bandit, come!" (Of course, if your ferret's name isn't Bandit, you should use his name instead.) The ferret's name should always come first, and the command must be the same every time. Be assertive when calling but use a cheerful, pleasant voice.

As the command is given by Person B, Person A releases Bandit making sure that he goes toward the stick. Constantly repeating the command, Person B gradually pulls the stick toward himself, enticing the pupil. In the best of circumstances, Bandit will actually follow the stick. When he reaches Person B, allow him to lick the skin and coat supplement off the spoon as a reward. Give him plenty of praise for a job well done. Now repeat the process, with Person B guiding Bandit and Person A holding the stick.

Maintain this two-foot distance between Person A and Person B for a few days of practice until Bandit consistently reaches his goal. Increase the distance to two and a half feet for a few more days. Then gradually extend this span by six-inch increments. This may not seem like fast progress, but the small increments are necessary so that Bandit won't realize he's covering more ground.

When Person A and Person B get to be three and a half feet apart, and the stick is only three feet long, what happens? Person A with the stick puts the spoon under Bandit's nose and then backs up the required distance, all the while luring the little guy along. After one or two months

Put a treat on the target stick and put it under the ferret's nose.

Lure the ferret with the treat while calling his name.

Give the ferret the treat when he reaches his goal.

of daily practice, it should be possible for Bandit to cover a distance of ten feet. Now's the time to stop putting the treat right under his nose. Instead, stand some distance away from him when you call his name. He might not be able to see the stick because ferrets don't have great eyesight, but he will be able to smell the reward because ferrets have an acute sense of smell. By now, Bandit should have the hang of things, and come running for a reward when you call his name. Now's the time to dispense with the stick and go just to the voice command "Bandit, come!"

While he's learning, it's important to give him a treat every time he comes; otherwise he'll stop responding. Once he's coming consistently, it's time to alter the reward schedule. Instead of giving Bandit a treat every time he comes to you, give him a reward every second or third time. This is known as *intermittent reward*, and animal behavior research shows that once a behavior is learned, intermittent rewards do a better job of reinforcing the behavior than rewarding it every single time.

Flying solo

So you don't have another family member or loyal friend who owes you big time? And you can't find someone to commit to three or four or five practice sessions daily? Don't worry! You and Bandit can go it alone.

You still need to make a target stick. But, instead of a second person, what you need is a harness and leash. (See Chapter 11 for information on how to fit a harness and choose a leash.) The training procedure is the same as already described; the only difference is that you yourself guide your ferret. When you put the spoon under his nose and give the command "Bandit, come!," gently pull on his leash so that he follows the stick as you draw it toward yourself. The leash prevents him from wandering away.

You have more control over your student when you use a leash, so it's very tempting to try longer distances sooner. Don't do it. Taking things in small stages, and repeating those steps frequently, is what ingrains the behavior. When do you get rid of the leash? That's a good question! When you reach the end of your rope (leash) and you see that Bandit's got the message, then it's time to let go.

Playing hooky

What happens when your kit isn't paying attention and wanders away during training? If he wanders even a smidgen, gently nab him before he makes the Great Escape and lead him right back to the stick. These sessions aren't playtime. Bandit has to know that this is school and not recess. If he runs away, bring him back to finish his homework. It will take only a few minutes anyhow.

However, if Bandit is really wound up and is refusing to cooperate, your best plan is to scrap the training session and go play together. Let your fuzzy run off some of his pent-up energy, and postpone the training until later in the day. After all, training is supposed to be fun . . . not an exercise in frustration.

If your ferret seems to have a really short attention span and has difficulty keeping his mind on the job, perhaps he's not the most gifted student in the class. Let's face it: Not all ferrets are equal when it comes to brainpower. With a slow learner, the main thing is not to get discouraged. Teach him what you can, and love him as he is.

Keep practice sessions short. You don't want to wear out your ferret.

Practice, practice, practice

Great ballet dancers practice hours every day, marathon runners train hours every day, concert pianists rehearse hours every day—not you and Bandit! You can accomplish great things with mere minutes of daily practice. Just how much is enough? Three to four short practice sessions a day are all it takes. Four five-minute sessions are much better than one twenty-minute session. Remember that a ferret has a short attention span on the best of days.

Don't hog the limelight. Let everyone in the household join in these practice sessions. Not only will it be fun, but your ferret will recognize the voices of everyone in the family and learn to respond to all of them.

Practice when perfect

So now your kit comes bounding with that little ferret dance every time you call—from the kitchen, from the dining room, and even from the upstairs bedroom. However, it's still important to reinforce his skills by daily practice, or as near daily as your busy life allows. It's also important to keep the rewards coming, even intermittently, because rewarding learned behavior is important, not only now but also two years down the road. As with other parts of your fuzzy's training, frequency and consistency are the keys to success.

Chapter Eight
Hide and Squeak

Where's the ferret?

The kids are fighting in the hallway, waiting to get to school, you're already fifteen minutes late for work, and your furry friend is nowhere in sight. Tempers are fraying, your blood pressure's rising, and that darn ferret isn't coming when called. She's somewhere deep in dreamland. Does this scenario sound familiar? You *know* that little bundle of energy shouldn't run loose in the house while you're gone, but you can't wait around any longer.

Save yourself this aggravation. The next time you're out picking up pet food, check out the squeaky toys. It's a rare ferret who doesn't respond to one of these toys—immediately! Most will even rouse themselves from a sound sleep to answer the call.

There is the odd ferret, however, that hates the sound of a squeaky toy and will nip anyone in the vicinity whenever she hears the sound. Does your furball get bitey when you squeak that toy? Then try a different sound. For example, you could put some pennies in a coffee can and give them a good shake.

Picking and choosing

Select your squeaky toy carefully. Many squeaky toys are available, but not all are suitable. What you're looking for is a stuffed toy with the squeaker hidden safely inside. Make sure that there are no pom-pom noses or plastic eyes that can be torn or ripped off. The squeaker itself should make a loud, high-pitched noise. Give them all a squeeze at the store to test them out. If you can, take your ferret with you. See what turns her on.

Pass right by the shelf with the cute rubber and latex toys. Your ferret will go crazy over these, but they're definitely on the danger list. If she gets her paws on one, or more likely her teeth, she could end up paying an unscheduled visit to the veterinarian.

Squeak and treat

After one squeak, most ferrets will automatically come running. Don't ask why; it just happens. The trick is to keep your pet coming to the squeak time after time. This is where rewards come in again! When she runs to the squeak, dole out a treat. Soon it'll be second nature—*squeak*–treat, *squeak*–treat, *squeak*–treat.

So, what can you do if your ferret's not a natural when it comes to a squeaky toy? It's rare, but it does happen. It's not a real problem; she can be taught what to do. Start by sitting in front of her with a treat. Make it a good one! Put the goodie under her nose and, as you squeak the toy, gradually entice her toward you. When she gets right to you, dole out the reward. Practice several times a day, gradually increasing the distance between you and your pet. You might find the target stick comes in handy here.

Soon you'll be able to stand in the kitchen (*squeak*), in the hallway (*squeak*), or in the bedroom (*squeak*), and your eager beaver will come running. She can even be snoring away, dead to the world, and she'll spring up and dash for her reward.

"Is that a squeak I hear?"

Knowing when to squeak

Your ferret's one smart cookie. If you squeak and treat only when you want to put her back into her cage, she'll soon figure out what you're up to and think twice about coming. So squeak for the good things in life too—kisses, cuddles, walks, romps—and she'll be sure to show up every time.

Because the toy works like magic (*squeak* and—presto—instant ferret), children might think it's great fun to *squeak*, *squeak*, *squeak* and watch their kit come scurrying as fast as her little legs can carry her. Or, you might be tempted to use it too often. Don't overdo it. It's not a game. It's a way of getting your pet to surface when you need her.

Just one squeak and Patch is on the ball.

Crossed signals?

Occasionally, when you use the toy, you'll notice that your able student doesn't put two and two together. She hears the squeak. She rushes for the treat. The trouble is that she rushes to the wrong person. There you are squeaking away in the kitchen while someone in the hallway has a ferret dancing at his feet. What's the problem? Your ferret has a one-track mind—gimme that goodie! So, in her excitement, she runs up to the first person she meets. To get her back on track, walk toward your baffled buddy and, when you're a few feet away, squeak again. She'll soon figure out who has the goods.

Lost and found

Indoors or out, a squeaky toy can be a lifesaver. If your ferret goes missing in the house, squeak in each room until she appears. If there's still no sign of her, she could be stuck somewhere. Squeak again and listen for her scrabbling. She may need to be rescued from a tight corner.

Should she escape from the house, get outside as soon as possible and squeak all over the neighborhood. If she's in earshot at all, she'll come for her treat. The squeaky toy is particularly helpful when a search party is out after dark. Even though you won't see her, she might hear you. And you might hear her if you keep your ears open for her bell.

Chapter Nine
Click and Treat

Clicking for results

In the previous chapter you learned how to use a squeaky toy to get a response from your ferret. In this chapter, you'll learn how to train your fuzzy by using a "clicking" sound. Clicker training is now one of the most popular and effective methods of teaching pets a whole variety of behaviors. Perhaps you've heard of clicker training being used with dogs. But did you know that the technique is used with all sorts of pets, including horses, cats, birds, rats, rabbits, fish, and hamsters? So why not give it a try with your ferret? To get started, all you need is a clicker and a supply of your furball's favorite treats.

Click-treat

It's best to start clicker training in a small ferret-proofed room where your fuzzy will have few distractions. Let him run off some of his energy so that he gets exploring out of his system and is more likely to pay attention. Now for the first step, which is really very simple. Sit down close to your pet with some treats in one hand and the clicker in the other. Next, press the clicker once and give your pet a treat right away. Then, continue to *click*-treat, *click*-treat, *click*-treat. That's the first step, known as *charging* or *loading* the clicker. This step gets the message across to your pet that a click equals a treat. The timing is important here. As soon as you click, give that fuzzy a treat. Immediately!

You're not trying to teach your ferret any specific behavior at this point;

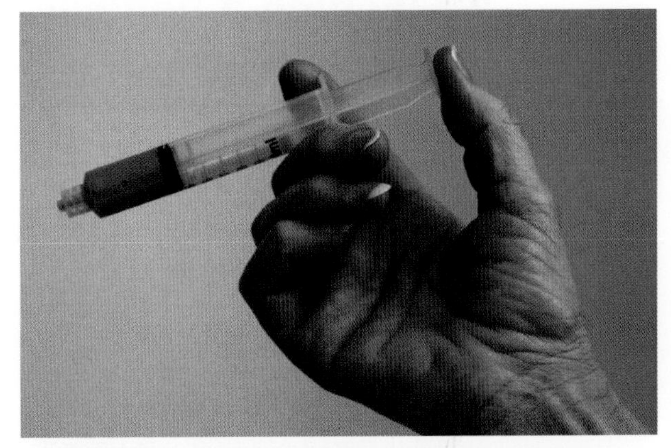

A needle-less syringe is useful for rewarding your fuzzy with tiny treats of baby-food meat or skin and coat supplement.

you're just getting him to associate the sound of the click with a reward. To do this, you need to *click*-treat at least ten times in quick succession. Keep the rewards small—a *lick* of skin and coat supplement, a *sliver* of ferret treat, a *dab* of baby-food meat—so that they can be swallowed almost immediately. Also, you don't want to overdo the treats because it's unhealthy for your ferret, and ferrets tend to lose interest in a treat if they get too much of it at once.

Repeat the charging of the clicker a couple of times a day for a few days until your ferret has made the association between the click and the reward. How will you know when he's made the connection? If your pet gets excited when you bring out the clicker, or comes running to you hopefully, as if to say, "Where's the treat? Where's the treat?," then he's got the message.

Teaching a behavior

As soon as your ferret knows that click = treat, it's time to move on to the next step—actually teaching him how to do something. One of the very easiest behaviors to teach with a clicker is rolling over. Here's what to do.

Begin by sitting on the floor with the clicker in your hand. Have several small treats handy, too, either in a fanny pack or in a bowl by your side. When you're teaching this particular skill, it's better to use tiny treats that you can hold in your fingers.

First, take a small piece of treat and put it in front of your ferret's nose where he can smell it. As soon as he sniffs at it, *click*-treat. Repeat this a few times. Next, instead of clicking and treating as soon as he sniffs at the reward, move it away from his nose, and around one side of his head toward his shoulder. When he follows your fingers and brings his head around, *click*-treat. Repeat this step several times. For the next step, start again from his nose, and bring your hand around one side of his head toward his shoulder, but this time go past his shoulder. When his head follows your hand, *click*-treat. And, again, repeat, repeat, repeat. Finally, starting from his nose, bring your hand around one side of his head, past his shoulder, and across his back so that he has to roll all the way over to get the treat. When he's completed the roll, *click*-treat, and repeat.

What you're actually doing is breaking up the behavior into small steps and clicking/rewarding each step of the way. This whole step-by-step process is known as shaping the behavior. Some ferrets will catch on right away, and will be rolling over in no time. Others will take longer to master each step and put them all together to come up with a roll.

Adding the cue

Once your ferret has got the hang of rolling over and is doing it consistently, it's time to add a command—

known in clicker training as the *cue*. The moment you start luring your pet into the roll with a treat, say, "Roll over!" or make a hand signal, such as tracing a circle in the air with your finger. Then, as soon as he completes the roll, click and treat.

Here's something to keep in mind. Each time you give your fuzzy a cue, give it only once. If you keep repeating the cue over and over, your ferret will think that "Roll over, roll over, roll over!" is the command, and won't perform until you've said it three times.

It might seem odd to wait until your pet is reliably performing a behavior before adding the command, but this is how it's done in clicker training. You ingrain the behavior first by clicking and treating; then when your ferret's doing exactly what you want, you add the cue.

Rewards are important in clicker training.

Dispensing with the clicker

Will you have to keep using the clicker when your ferret has learned to roll on cue? The answer is no. As soon as your pet is rolling over on command, then it's time to stop using the clicker to mark *that* behavior and start using it to teach a new behavior. In clicker training, the clicker is reserved for teaching new behaviors or for reteaching a skill that your fuzzy has forgotten.

Even when you've dispensed with the clicker, you need to keep handing out rewards. However, you don't need to give them every single time your ferret responds to a cue. You could try giving intermittent rewards as described on page 44. For some ferrets the reward could be a tummy tickle or a special toy, but most fuzzies prefer a food treat.

Begging behavior

Some ferrets are pretty smart. As soon as they realize that rolling over gets them a treat, these ferret smart-

Do's and don'ts of clicker training

- DO practice in an area where there are no distractions.
- DO speak nicely to your pet.
- DO keep training sessions short—quit before your furball is bored.
- DO keep training sessions fun.
- DO reward immediately after every click.
- DO keep the clicker away from children. If a child *click-click-clicks*, your ferret will become confused, and months of training will go down the tubes.

- DON'T start a training session when your ferret's just eaten.
- DON'T scold or punish a pet during clicker training.
- DON'T click more than once each time.
- DON'T click the clicker in your pet's face. You might startle him into nipping you.
- DON'T holler out your cues.
- DON'T use the clicker outside of training sessions.

alecks start rolling over and over at every opportunity in hopes of getting a reward. Although this begging behavior can be cute at first, over time it can become really annoying. You can't prevent begging from starting, but you can stop it. How? Reward only cued behavior. "No cue, no reward" should be your motto.

Keep clicking

Rolling over isn't the only thing you can train your pet to do with a clicker. Clicker training has been used successfully to teach ferrets a whole range of behaviors, including sitting up, coming when called, litter training, going into the cage at night, running through a tunnel, and more. Just use the same basic method:

- Get your pet to perform a desired behavior, either by catching him in the act (for example, when he's running through a tunnel) or by luring him with a treat (such as when you want him to roll over).
- Shape the behavior bit by bit, marking each step with a click.
- The moment you click, reward with a treat.
- When your pet is reliably performing the behavior, add the cue.

Has this short introduction to clicker training got you motivated to turn your furball into a clicker pro? Although not a lot has been written about how to clicker train ferrets, there are lots of books and web sites that explain how to clicker train dogs and other animals. The techniques described in these guides can easily be adapted for ferrets.

Chapter Ten

Special Needs—Special Training

Hard of hearing but not hard to train

All the squeaking and clicking in the world won't do the slightest bit of good if your ferret is deaf. Deafness in ferrets is more common than you might think. Many Panda and Blaze ferrets, and some dark-eyed whites, are born deaf because of an inherited disorder called Waardenburg Syndrome. Other ferrets lose their hearing through ear-mite infestation, illness, or aging. Fortunately, there's no need to give up on training deaf ferrets. You just have to modify your techniques a little.

Before training

Before you can even begin training a hearing-impaired ferret, there is one important point to keep in mind. Always approach your pet slowly from the front so that she can see you coming. If you grab a deaf ferret from behind, she's liable to be startled and start screaming or nipping out of fear. If she's sleeping, try blowing on her fur to rouse her rather than just scooping her up and startling her. Don't blow in her face, though. She won't like it.

Vibration rather than sound

Although you'll probably find yourself talking to your deaf ferret, obviously she's not going to hear you. But, surprisingly enough, if you hold your fuzzy right against your body, she'll feel the vibrations of your chest as you sing or talk. Many deaf ferrets enjoy this sensation, as it gives them a feeling of security. It's a great way to bond with a deaf buddy.

There are also many practical ways to use vibration rather than sound when training a deaf ferret. For example, you can use vibration to attract her attention. If she's in her cage, try tapping on the cage wires

A Blaze ferret has a white stripe on its head. Many of them are deaf.

to let her know that it's time to come out. Of course, she won't hear the tapping, but she'll feel the vibrations running through the cage.

Once she's out of her cage, you can use vibration to encourage your ferret to come to you. Many owners find that knocking or stomping on the floor produces good results. This is especially true if the floor is wood, laminate, or linoleum. With carpeted floors, it might be necessary to get closer to the fuzzy before she can feel the vibrations. If her natural curiosity doesn't bring her running, or if she scoots off in the opposite direction, try bribing her with a treat. If you repeat *stomp*-treat, *stomp*-treat, *stomp*-treat, she'll soon catch on.

If knocking or stomping isn't getting results, here's something else to try. Invest in a handheld, battery-operated mini-massager—the type used for kneading neck and shoulder muscles. Turn it on and press it against the floor; your pet will feel the vibrations. At the same time, hold up a treat. It won't be long before your fuzzy realizes that when she feels that peculiar sensation, she'll get a reward when she comes to you.

Flash-treat

One of the most effective ways to train a deaf ferret is with a flashlight. Just follow the instructions given in Chapter 9 for clicker training, but instead of using a clicker to let your ferret know she's done what you wanted, use a small key-chain flashlight with an instant on/off press button. What do you do with the flashlight? You use it to *flash*-treat rather than *click*-treat. One short flash is all that's necessary to mark the completion of a desired behavior. Make sure your ferret can see the flash, but don't shine the light in her eyes. And don't use a laser pointer; a rambunctious ferret might bounce in front of the strong light beam and damage her eyes.

When flashlight training has progressed to the point of adding a cue, you'll probably find yourself using a voice command automatically. Unfortunately, this won't do much good unless your ferret can read lips. So you'll have to remember to use a hand signal instead of a verbal cue. Each behavior you teach will need a separate hand signal, and the signals should be distinct so they can't be confused with one another. For example, the cue for "Come" could be holding your hand out flat, with the palm up, and then moving your fingers back and forth towards your wrist. And the cue for "Roll over" could be sketching a circle in the air with your finger.

Flashlight training works really well with deaf ferrets. With daily practice, a deaf ferret can learn anything by the *flash*-treat method that a hearing ferret can be taught by the *click*-treat method.

Blind or sight-impaired ferrets

Sometimes owners don't realize that their bouncy little furball has a vision problem. That's because blind ferrets have an uncanny knack of learning their way around their environment. By depending on their other senses, like smell and touch, they can compensate for the loss of

A hearing-impaired ferret can feel you tapping on her cage.

Suzie is sight-impaired, but this doesn't stop her!

sight. But if you notice that your fuzzy keeps bumping into furniture or falling over toys, you should take her to the veterinarian and have her checked for vision problems.

With a blind ferret in the house, there are a few things you should keep in mind. First and foremost, don't startle that fuzzy! Never pick her up without giving some sort of sound signal . . . a reassuring word, a song, or a whistle. And if you have other ferrets in your household, attach bells to their collars or harnesses so that they can't sneak up and surprise her.

How else can you make life easier for a blind ferret? Don't rearrange the furniture, and avoid clutter in the play area. You might also need to do some extra ferret-proofing, such as blocking off stairways to prevent the blind ferret from falling between the railings.

And what about training blind ferrets? The fact is, even sighted ferrets don't have the greatest vision, so blind ferrets aren't at a great disadvantage. Most of them can be trained to do everything that a sighted ferret can do, using the same techniques. Just make sure that in any treat-based training, the treat is within smelling distance since your pet won't be able to see it.

Chapter Eleven
Walking on a Leash

Take a walk on the wild side

That's exactly what you'll be doing if your ferret isn't properly trained to walk on a leash. He'll dart under, over, and in front of your feet. You'll be doing wild dances in the street to avoid stepping on the poor thing. You could even injure him if you misjudge your step. Dragging him down the street on a six-inch leash isn't the answer. Of course, you could always leave him home and forget the walks, but you don't have to give up. Just put him through his paces for a couple of weeks, and before you know it, you'll be parading proudly through the neighborhood.

A Lassie he won't be. Heeling, stopping, or staying on command won't ever be part of his repertoire. But he can learn to walk at your side without getting tangled up in your toes. When he's mastered the following techniques, be prepared for approving glances and admiring comments.

All kitted out

Before you hit the streets, you'll need to invest in a harness and a leash. Choosing a leash is easy. There are lots available made specifically for ferrets. Or you could buy a kitten leash, or even a retractable leash. Try to find something with a swivel hook at the end—the swivel prevents the leash from getting twisted and tangled. Check with your ferret about his color preference.

For walking outdoors, a ferret needs a harness and leash.

Ferrets are real escape artists when it comes to collars; they can slip out of them very easily. So, when you're walking your pet, he *must* wear a harness. It's well worth your while to look for one of the excellent ferret harnesses on the market. Or, you might find something suitable in kitten supplies. And for the fashion-conscious ferret, there are even designer ferret harnesses available now. What you need is a harness that is easy to put on your ferret. It has to provide room for growth, but it must be a snug fit for your kit. How snug is snug? You should be able to get the tip of your baby finger, but no more, under the straps. If the harness is any tighter, you'll strangle him; if it's any looser, you'll lose him. For the perfect fit, try before you buy.

Remember that your ferret is very low to the ground. Any dangling straps, which might trip him, should be trimmed, leaving an inch or two for growth. If the harness is nylon, hold the cut end to a lighted match. This will melt the end and stop it from fraying. Smooth any sharp edges while the nylon is still warm and pliable.

Getting the feel of things

If your kit fusses about wearing his new harness, do yourself a favor and don't bother putting it on until he's past the baby stage. It's not worth the fight. When he's a little older and more amenable to wearing one, he'll need to spend some time indoors getting used to it. Buckle him up a couple of times a day and let him run around for half an hour. You'll have fun watching him adjust to his new gear.

After a few days, attach the leash, hold on to it, and see how your kit reacts. He may not like it at first. In fact, he may even try to bite through it. A little perseverance and a few squirts of bitter spray on the leash will soon discourage him. The great advantage to starting indoors is that you can make sure his harness is tight enough to prevent escape before you face the great outdoors.

Fit your ferret's harness so he's comfortable but can't slip out.

Right on target

Remember that invaluable piece of equipment, the target stick? Remember how you used it to teach your ferret to come when called? Well, now's the time to get it out again. To turn it into a dual-purpose stick, you'll have to add another piece. There's already a plastic spoon taped to one end. Take an identical spoon and tape it to the other end at a right angle to the stick. The finished product should look like a golf club.

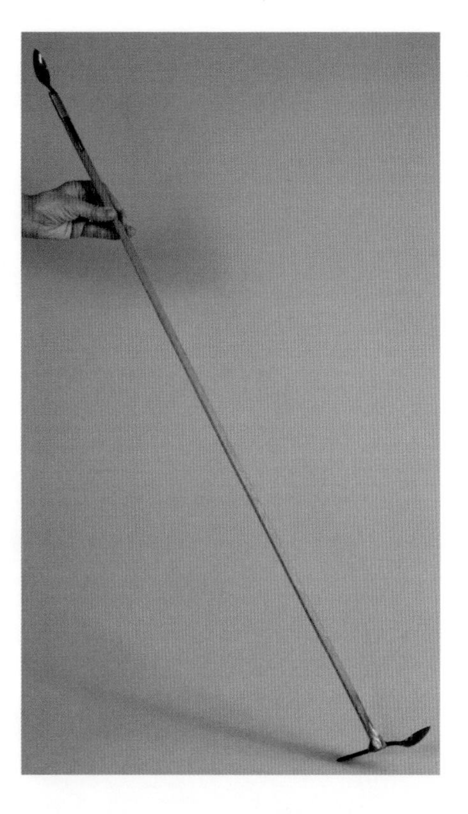

Add another plastic spoon to your target stick, and you can start leash training.

On your mark, get set, go!

Now that the harness is properly fitted and your stick is ready, it's time to graduate to the outdoors. First, determine which side you want your ferret to walk on, right or left. Don't switch at your fancy—your ferret will only get confused. Choose whichever side is comfortable for you and stick with it. Most right-handed people prefer the left side, which is the traditional one for walking pets.

Start by taking the leash in your left hand. If necessary, shorten it up by wrapping it around your palm. This keeps your pet beside you so he can't wander from the straight and narrow. Prime the spoon with a few drops of skin and coat supplement and take hold of the stick with your right hand.

The game plan is simple. Put the spoon directly in front of your ferret's nose, but just out of reach—tempting and tantalizing, close enough for him to see it and smell it, but not close enough to taste it. Walking slowly, with the stick held slightly ahead of him, coax your ferret along a distance of one foot. Then give him his reward. Beware of cheating—you'll be surprised how long his tongue is! Repeat the sequence several times, encouraging his efforts in a pleasant, firm voice, and that's enough for the first practice. As always, the more short practices you can work in per day, the better.

Start with the treat under your pet's nose . . .

. . . entice him to walk along by your side . . .

. . . a little farther yet . . .

. . . then give the reward.

Maintain the one-foot distance for the next few days and then gradually increase the distance a foot at a time. Don't try to hurry the progress even if your ferret seems capable of going farther faster. It's frequent practices over short distances that will have your pet pounding the pavement in no time.

Noise shy

Hoots, hollers, honks, slams, sirens, squeals, birds, barks, and backfires are just a few of the sudden sounds that might startle your buddy on your daily walks together. And on holidays or special occasions, what about firecrackers, noisemakers, and bursting balloons? If your ferret jumps suddenly, if his fur stands on end and he starts to scuttle backward, you can be sure he's frightened. It's important to be aware that your pet can be scared easily by loud noises, especially if he's purchased in the winter and spends most of his first few months indoors. Crowds can also be scary. From a ferret's-eye view, all those feet look like a stampede. For safety in a crowd, use a carrier. (See Chapter 13.)

Don't keep yanking your pet along when he's scared. Gently scoop him up. Speak to him in a reassuring voice and soothe him by cuddling and petting. Carry him along for a while before you put him down again. As he has more frequent exposure to strange noises, he'll gradually become desensitized to them.

Try the park for a change of scene.

There are, however, some scaredy cats who never enjoy being outside. The sights and sounds are just too overwhelming. If, after a determined effort, you find that your ferret isn't enjoying the outdoors, don't force him. Give him his daily exercise indoors and avoid a lot of frustration for both of you.

Take the rough with the smooth

Introduce your ferret to a wide variety of surfaces—cool damp grass, loose gritty gravel, soft moist dirt, smooth hard pavement, rough uneven brick. That way he won't balk at changing terrain and will be much more versatile in where you can take him. Whatever the terrain, keep your eye on the ground. Did the neighbor's kid leave a balloon

A warm coat keeps out winter chills.

lying about or drop a rubber band? While you're walking with your head in the clouds, your ferret could be pouncing on unexpected treasures at your feet. If you frequently walk your pet on hard surfaces, he may require extra foot care. Pamper those paw pads. To prevent drying out and cracking, apply a moisturizer regularly. Whenever you put lotion on your hands, rub some into your ferret's feet!

Winter woes

There's a foot of snow outside, an icy blast greets you at the door, and your buddy is sitting there, leash in mouth, ready to go. Now what do you do? If the weather is extremely cold, it isn't reasonable to think about going outside for a walk. You could, however, take a tour of your house or apartment, or use your basement as an indoor track. Remember, any indoor walking is better than no practice at all.

If, however, the winter weather is suitable for walking, there are some precautions to keep in mind. Because a house ferret isn't used to outside temperatures, your pet will need a warm sweater or coat. If you can't find one locally, search the Internet, where you'll find lots of sweaters, jackets, sweatshirts, and parkas designed specifically for a ferret's long body and short legs.

A winter wonderland can be a perfect playground for your ferret. He'll love to slip, slide, and tunnel in

A soft towel warms your ferret after a winter's walk.

the snow, clucking like crazy as he chases snowballs and snowflakes. Just don't overdo it. Be careful that his feet don't get too cold or his fur too wet. When you bring him back inside after a winter romp, give him a brisk rub in a fluffy towel. Sneezes and sniffles aren't restricted to two-footed walkers.

Cold temperatures aren't the only winter worry. Road and sidewalk salt can cause serious burns on your ferret's foot pads. Never allow your pet to walk on salted streets or sidewalks. And always wash off his feet after a winter stroll to remove any traces of salt or grit.

Summer sweats

Would you take a walk in the heat of summer, muffled from head to toe in a fur coat? Of course you wouldn't! Your ferret won't relish the idea either. If you're not careful, heat exhaustion can threaten your pet's life. In very warm weather it may be better to confine your walks to the early morning or the cool of the evening. Another good idea if you're out for long is to carry a freezer pack with you. Your ferret can lie on it to cool off. Use common sense in gauging how far your ferret can walk comfortably. If he shows *any* signs

Patch skinny-dipping on a hot summer's day.

of discomfort while walking in the summer, get him out of the heat immediately.

For your ferret, a walk when it's warm may be like running a race. So carry a small bottle of fresh water on your summer strolls and be sure to offer him periodic drinks. If he won't drink from the bottle or bottle cap, try getting him to lick the water from your finger.

Think of the last time you skipped across a parking lot or beach in the scorching summer heat with bare feet—ouch! Ferrets don't wear shoes and have no way of telling you that the sidewalk is hot. You have to be the judge of what's safe and comfortable for his tender tootsies.

After his walk, why not let him have a dip in his own private pool? A cheap plastic pool or baby bath is ideal. Many ferrets enjoy an occasional swim in a few inches of water as long as the water isn't too cold. Forget the laps in the family pool, though. The chemicals aren't safe for him. He shouldn't take dips in the ocean, either. Swallowing salt water is hazardous to his health.

Keep off the grass

WARNING PESTICIDE USE—you must have seen these signs around your neighborhood. They are meant not only for people but also for pets. Think about how your ferret rolls and slithers through the grass, sniffing every blade. If the grass has just been sprayed with weed killer, pesticides, or fertilizer, then it isn't the grass your ferret should be playing in. The chemicals could be a health risk. So, if you see a sign indicating the recent use of toxic sprays, pick up your pet and walk elsewhere.

Ferrets don't sweat. To protect your pet from heat stress, keep him cool when the temperature rises.

Other herbaceous hazards to avoid include poison ivy, cacti, and nettles. You'll know the plants to look out for in your part of the country. As a general rule, whatever you should avoid, your ferret should avoid. Calamine lotion might be a fine remedy for people suffering from poison ivy, but it's a bit hard to get it through a thick coat of ferret fur!

Those pesky pests

Any furry pet walking outside has the chance of catching every pet owner's nightmare—fleas! Not only are these little bugs pesky for your kit, but they can also turn your carpeting into Fleatown overnight. Be constantly on the lookout for fleas when grooming your ferret. If you notice any, get rid of them by using a flea shampoo made for ferrets or cats, but stay away from flea collars, dips, and dog products.

Do you live in a part of the country where fleas are a real problem? Then be proactive and check out flea prevention products. Some of these come in spray form, some are given orally, and some are rubbed into the skin. Some are prescription only, and some can be bought over the counter. None of them are ferret-specific, but the cat formulas are often recommended for ferrets. Ask your veterinarian which product is best for your pet.

Mosquitoes can also be a problem. Not only are they a nuisance, but they can also infect your pet with

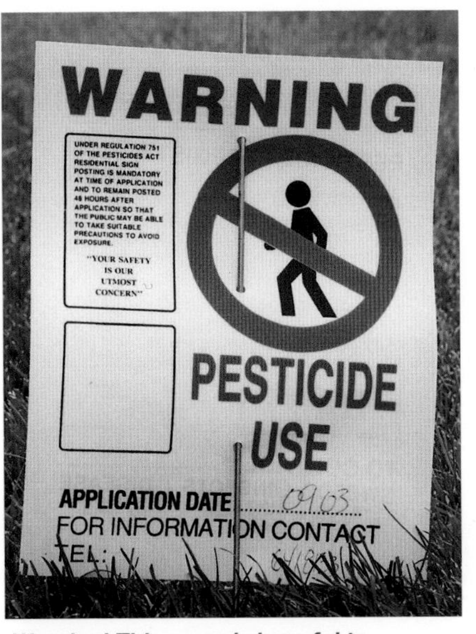

Warning! This grass is harmful to ferrets, too.

heartworm. Ask your veterinarian whether this disease is prevalent in your area and, if so, ask about preventive medicine. This comes in liquid form and tablet form, but it's better to get the liquid because it's easier to get it into your ferret. Just mix it with some skin and coat supplement, and your pet will lap it up.

There are some combination medications on the market that protect pets against fleas, ticks, heartworms, ear mites, and mange. These are available by prescription only, so again, consult with your veterinarian.

Scoop the poop

The last few paragraphs have all addressed environmental hazards that could affect your pet. However, your pet could be the environmental hazard unless you carry a trusty pooper-scooper for cleanups. Be a responsible pet owner and take along a small plastic bag and some tissues for potty stops.

Beware of the dog

Be alert on your walks. Scan the horizon; look 'fore and aft. What you're watching for is trouble—in the shape of dogs, particularly the unleashed variety with no visible owner. Even dogs on a leash can pose a danger if they like to chase small furry creatures. When you see a leashed dog, cross the street or pick up your ferret and pass by at a distance. It's better to be safe than sorry.

Stray dogs are a more serious matter; there's no owner around to control them. If you round a corner and find yourself face to face with a roving runaway, don't assume the dog will go merrily on its way and ignore you both. Take immediate action to protect your ferret. Grab him and stuff him into your shirt, coat, or whatever to get him out of the dog's sight. Quickly put as much distance as possible between you and the stray. If it persists in following you, make a beeline for the nearest neighbor, shop, or place of safety.

Where strays are a real problem, the best defense may be a good offense. An effective product to have in hand if you come eyeball to eyeball with a menacing mutt is a mild, dog-repellent, pepper spray. Letter carriers and joggers use this spray as protection against fierce canines. It's a humane deterrent, causing discomfort but no actual harm. Aim for the dog's face when you spray, making sure you and your ferret are out of range. Then beat a retreat. If this measure seems somewhat extreme, just remember that your ferret might look like lunch to a hungry stray. An aggressive dog that means business could pose a very real threat to you and your pet.

Cats are easier to deal with. If you find your ferret being stalked by a tenacious tabby, take offensive action. Pick up and protect your ferret and then scat that cat. Cats, dogs, and ferrets can get along together quite happily in the same house. It's unexpected encounters that spell trouble. The bottom line is—it's better never to take a chance with a strange dog or cat.

Strolling down the avenue

So now you and your ferret are part of the neighborhood scene. These walks with your buddy are bringing you double takes, eager questions, and new friends. They are giving him the opportunity for snooping, sniffing, romping, and rollicking. Enjoy your strolls together; take time to smell the roses. This is your reward for work well done!

Chapter Twelve

Fun and Games

All work and no play

All work and no play makes Jill a dull girl! Because your ferret alternates between long hours of sleep and furious bursts of activity, play is important as an outlet for her energies. It gives her the exercise she needs and alleviates boredom. Playtime is just as important as formal training time. A ferret learns by playing. This is how she improves her social skills and finds out what's acceptable and what's not. Play develops trust and encourages bonding. Ferrets love to play—it's part of being a ferret.

People games

Playing with your ferret will bring out the kid in you. All the games you loved as a child are natural ferret fun. Take tag, for example. This is on the top-ten list. Chase your ferret around the house or apartment, gently tap her tail, and then encourage her to chase you. She'll soon pick up the idea, and you'll both be romping through the rooms, laughing and clucking.

Hide-and-seek is a big hit. Ferrets know instinctively how to play this game. When your rascal runs and hides under the sofa, go looking for her, calling out, "Jill, where are you?" Imitate her "dooking" sounds and announce, "Ready or not, here I come!" Act excited when you find her, and she'll happily run to another hiding place. Who cares if you look foolish?

Give peek-a-boo a try. When your ferret runs under the sofa or chair, gently tap at the bottom skirt. She'll stick her nose out and sniff. Sing, "Peek-a-boo!" as you *gently* rub her nose. Tap the skirt at a different spot. She'll scurry over to it and stick out the tip of her nose again. Surprisingly, she'll keep this up for quite a while, scooting from spot to spot as you tap.

Tug-of-war is another winner. This is an easy one. Hold one end of an old towel and give your ferret the other. She'll latch on immediately, pulling and tugging, trying to get it away from you. She'll swirl and roll around, grabbing with her paws, giving it her best shot. Be gentle, though—broken teeth are hard to fix. And watch out! After she gets the hang of this game, she might yank at anything that dangles—shirts on door knobs, sheets over the bed, towels in the bathroom. How's she to know the difference between the play towel and your best guest towel?

Another game ferrets can't resist is mock combat. It involves getting on the floor with your ferret and letting her pounce on your hand. Move your hand around and she'll chase it. Tickle her tummy and she'll jump up and pounce on your hand again. Now she's doing the ferret war dance—springing around, back hunched, fur bristled. No, she's not on the attack; she's just having fun. Be sure to keep this game playful. If it becomes too rough, it needs to stop.

While you and your ferret are engaged in mock combat, why not lob a few sock bombs? Gently toss balled-up socks in Jill's direction and watch her leap to intercept them. If you make your bed the battleground, Jill can hide under cover between bomb attacks.

Ferret bowling will get your furball clucking for sure. The trick is to be *gentle* and *easy*. Find a laneway of smooth, polished floor space, cleared of all obstacles. Pick up and support your ferret with both hands. Point her posterior in the desired direction and, saying, "One, two, three!," send her sliding along the floor on her tummy. She'll come running back for more and more and more!

Bouncing balls

Ping-pong balls are great for starters. Bounce a few at a time on a hard floor and watch your pet go scuttling every which way. She'll grab a ball with her front paws, roll around and around, jump up, bat at the ball, and then chase it. For a change of pace, attach one to a string and swing it in front of her. Or, fill a box with ping-pong balls, toss her in, stand back, and watch the dance. A ball or two in the cage helps beat boredom. They're safe as long as they're not dented. Throw any dented ones into a cup of boiling water to make them as good as new. Toss out any cracked ones.

Natural rope or sisal balls are a good choice, as are tennis balls, but

Ping-pong balls make great ferret toys.

Your fuzzy will have a ball with a ferret ball.

golf balls are too hard. Don't offer sponge, rubber, or super balls, please. Anything that could have a piece bitten off is off-limits for your pet. Don't be discouraged if your little darling loses interest in her ball. Ferrets can be elated with a toy one minute and drop it abruptly the next. However, if you include a ferret treat ball in the toy box, your fuzzy is more likely to stay interested . . . at least until she rolls all the treats out!

Just for ferrets

Toys geared just to ferrets are popping up all over. Ferret balls are large and hollow with holes for investigating. You can even buy colored plastic see-through tunnels that attach to the balls to make a maze.

There are several brands of chew-treat toys made just for ferrets. Why not tie one of these to a shoestring, dangle it in front of your furball's nose, and get her to chase it? Ferret bounce-back toys are another winner. You can put treats in them, or rub them with scented candle wax to make them more interesting. Try this

Spoil your pets with special ferret toys.

A plastic shopping bag is the all-time ferret favorite.

scented-wax trick with balls, tunnels, and other ferret toys. It's a cheap way to enrich your pet's playtime.

In the cage or out, hammocks, bungee toys, and hanging tubes will keep your ferret amused. Soft material tubes and tents can round out the playground.

Not exactly a toy, but still lots of fun is the large selection of fashionable ferret wear that's now available. With hats, coats, biker and jean jackets, sweaters, T-shirts, and bandanas, your pet can be the best-dressed ferret on the block. And don't forget her Halloween costume and Santa suit.

Filched from Fido, captured from Kitty

Why let Fido and Kitty have all the fun? Some dog and cat toys such as dog tug ropes, cat balls, and crinkly cat bags and tunnels are just the thing for ferrets. However, let the buyer beware! Some cat and dog toys are *not* suitable because they won't stand up to a ferret's roughhousing. Stay away from toys with feathers, buttons, pom-poms, leather, and rawhide. If it can be pulled off, bitten off, chewed off, or gnawed off, it's a sure bet your ferret will take it off.

Choices, choices, choices . . . there's lots of cute clothing for the fashion-conscious ferret.

Hammocks are great for sleep or play.

Homemade treasures

Here's good news for ferret owners! Some of the best-loved, most enduring, and certainly cheapest play toys for ferrets are not store-bought at all. They're homemade treasures devised from everyday items you have on hand. The all-time favorite is a plastic shopping bag with the handles cut off—not a dry cleaning or bread bag. Your pet will spend hours (okay, minutes) rooting around inside the bag. She'll have double the fun if you join the game. Roll her around in the bag, drag her gently across the floor, and listen to her cluck. Better yet, bring out a pile of bags and let her dive right in. Warning! If you have a ferret who loves to eat plastic, these bags are not safe. Put a few ping-pong balls inside a paper bag instead and get the camcorder out!

Do you have a large plastic milk or water jug headed for the recycling bin? Recycle it instead to your pet's toy box. Cut several holes in it and let your ferret's imagination do the rest. Do you have any plastic two-liter pop bottles? Cut off the tops and bottoms and then cover the sharp edges at both ends with masking or duct tape—instant tunnel fun! Cut the legs off old sweatpants or jeans—more tunnel fun!

Dig, dig, dig! Fun, fun, fun! A clean plastic storage bin about six to eight inches high makes a great ferret sandbox. Pour in two to three inches of fresh sandbox sand, or a mixture of sand and potting soil. Then cut out a sizable hole in the lid or the side—one that's large enough for your ferret to get in and out of. It won't take long for your fuzzy to find the hole. To make things more interesting, why not add some ping-pong balls for a treasure hunt?

Don't want to clean up a lot of dirt? Then use regular rice (not instant) or starch packing pellets instead of dirt or sand. The starch pellets don't weigh much, so you can put them in a cardboard box instead of spending money on a plastic bin. But never use Styrofoam peanuts; they're bad for your pet if ingested.

A plastic bin is also good for ice-cube bobbing. Pour in an inch of tepid water, add a handful of ice cubes, and watch your fuzzy nab them! In the wintertime, you can even put snow in the bin for snow snorkeling.

Packaged entertainment

What household doesn't have boxes, boxes, and more boxes lying around? Don't throw out that empty cereal box. It makes a handy ferret wagon. Punch a hole in one end of the box, reinforce it with tape, and attach a long shoestring. Let your ferret crawl inside and pull her around—free ferret transportation! Don't go too fast, though. You don't want a speeding ticket.

Is that an empty shoe box? No, it's a new hidey-hole. Tape down the top and cut a circular hole out of one end. Throw in a few ping-pong balls followed by the ferret. Ferret will clatter; balls will scatter.

After grocery shopping, save all your empty cardboard pop-can boxes for ferret playtime. Just put a collection of them on the floor and leave your ferret to do the rest. As above, toss in a few ping-pong balls . . . dook, dook, cluck, cluck.

Do you have a few bored kids hanging around? A box maze for the ferret is just the project for a rainy afternoon. Any combination of boxes will do—tissue boxes, cereal boxes, cracker boxes—the more the merrier.

The ultimate ferret favorite

What's inexpensive, a snap to make, and at the top of the ferret favorite list? It's the terrific tube tunnel. Your ferret will love this toy because it gives her a chance to do what comes naturally—hide and tunnel. You'll love it because it's cheap, no tools are needed, and you can make it even if your fingers are all thumbs. Pick an afternoon or evening when everything on TV is boring and trot down to your nearest building supply center for the following materials:

- four sections of plastic corrugated drainage tubing (also known as weeping tile). Be sure to get the kind without holes, as ferret toenails can get stuck in the holes. Each section should be four inches

in diameter and two to three feet in length. Have the salesclerk cut it to size.

- two elbow connectors.
- one T-connector.
- one piece of medium grade sandpaper. (Hey, this isn't a tool!)

When you get home with the goods, here's what you do.

- Smooth the rough edges of the cut tubing with the sandpaper.
- Snap tubing sections into connectors.

That's all there is to it. A few minutes work for you; hours of fun for your ferret. Everything can be easily taken apart and rearranged to give your pet a new challenge. As time and money permit, you can add more tubing and connectors to expand the subway system. For more crazy capers, try dangling a chew treat into the T-connector or throw in a few ping-pong balls.

A change for the better

Ferrets have a short attention span, and will quickly tire of a toy. So, it's important to have a variety of toys around the house, and to keep changing the selection. Providing different toys is a way to stimulate your ferret's curiosity and enrich her emotional life. This doesn't mean that you have to keep running out to buy new playthings. You can search the Internet for ideas for more homemade toys. You can also put away some of your pet's current toys, and reintroduce them after a few weeks. This way, your fuzzy will *think* she's getting something new!

Chapter Thirteen

The Perfect Portable Pet

On the go

Ferrets love being around people. They also enjoy seeing the sights and exploring new places. What's a better way to do this than right along with you? As you go about your errands, picking up the mail, going to the library, and dropping off the dry cleaning, take your pet with you. His life will be more interesting when he meets people and goes places. And you'll enjoy his company. However, it's not always practical to haul him along with you on a leash; nor is it always safe—he could get stepped on in a crowd. For worry-free outings, why not check out a carry bag or a pet stroller?

Purchased pouches

When looking for a carry bag, the ones made just for ferrets are worth hunting for. Your local pet shop might not stock a wide variety, but you can find lots of different types advertised on the Internet. There are backpacks, front packs, purse-style bags, and couture creations. Some are made of canvas or nylon; some are soft and fleecy; some are plush and padded. Choices, choices, choices!

When your pet's in a front pack, you can keep an eye on him.

For the modern ferret-on-the-go, a pet stroller could be a practical pick. These are ideal for transporting sick ferrets, older ferrets, or kits that can't go far on a leash but would enjoy some fresh air. They're also handy if you have several ferrets and can't cram them all into a single carry bag. Some of these pet strollers are multipurpose; they are actually detachable pet carriers on a stroller frame. So, they can be used as strollers, as separate pet carriers, or as car carriers, complete with seat-belt loops.

When choosing a carry bag or pet stroller, check very carefully for any foam or rubber that could be a danger to your ferret. Remember, ferrets like to eat foam and rubber, so be sure to do a careful inspection of any product that you're planning to purchase.

A backpack can double as a ferret carry bag. But you can't see what your pet's up to, so clip him in with a short leash.

Check out your closet

On a tight budget? It might not be necessary to buy a carry bag—there could be something in your closet that you can press into service. For example, some backpacks are roomy enough for a hitchhiker, as are some shoulder bags and large purses. Gym bags with shoulder straps and adequate ventilation are another possibility.

An infant snuggle sack with the leg openings stitched up will also work. If you like to sew, browse through the pattern books under crafts or accessories for something suitable. Or, take a piece of fleece-backed material approximately thirty inches by fifteen inches, fold it in half, and stitch up the side seams. Add a shoulder strap and you're all set. A pocket on the pouch is an added bonus. It's a perfect place to pack food, water, and walking leash. Remember that your ferret needs to eat and drink frequently, and your outings may take longer than planned. Take along a cold pack in the summer in case the weather turns hot.

Whatever type of carrier you opt for, make sure it is sturdy and washable, roomy and comfortable, with nothing rubber, plastic, or sponge hidden inside. Toss in a favorite blankie, and you're ready to go.

Jack-in-the-box

You pop him in, he jumps out. You pop him in again, he jumps out again. You'll never get anywhere this way! How do you persuade your pet to stay put? Never fear; it just takes a little indoor practice—and a little bribery. Whip out his favorite goodie. Put him in his carrier and, as you stroll around the house, dole out tiny tidbits. Pat him on the head; tell him what a good boy he is. Every time he starts to struggle, say "NO!" in a firm voice and settle him back in the carrier with another bit of treat. Make the treat last so that he stays in the carrier for longer and longer periods. Pretty soon he'll enjoy his daily rides.

A short leash attached to the carry bag will stop your ferret from bailing out.

An ounce of prevention

Just in case your bold adventurer is tempted to bail out of his carry bag, a simple addition to it can prevent some anxious moments. A short, permanent leash inside the bag will keep him from escaping. This is especially helpful if your hands are full and he makes a bid for freedom. If you purchased a made-for-ferrets carry bag, it might already have a safety leash sewn inside. If it doesn't, or if you're using some other type of bag, you can easily install one. Here's how.

Buy a cheap, narrow leash with a swivel hook at one end. Make a mark on the leash twelve inches up from the hook and cut the leash at this point. Pass a lighted match over the cut edge if the leash is nylon, or dip the end in clear fingernail polish if the leash is cloth. This will prevent any fraying. Then sew this end inside your ferret's carrier along a seam.

Where exactly in the carrier you attach the leash—top, bottom, or middle—depends on the type of bag you've chosen. What you're aiming for is to have the leash long enough to give your pet freedom of movement but not so long that he gets tangled up. If a twelve-inch leash is too long, shorten it a bit. A cheaper solution is to buy narrow polypropylene tape or rope (from the fabric store) and a small swivel hook (from the hardware store) and make your own leash. Whichever route you take, your next step is to put your pet in his harness, plop him in his carrier, and clip on the leash. Now when he tries to hop out, he won't get far.

Watch for the wiggles

Is your ferret trying his darndest to get out of his carry bag? He may have a legitimate reason. More often than not, persistent wiggles mean potty time. You'll have to get him out of the bag, clip on his regular leash and let him do his business. Have tissues and plastic bags in your pocket to clean up any mess.

Take me out to the ball game

You can take your pet almost anywhere—the hockey arena, the football stadium, the skating rink, or the soccer field. How about picnics, garage sales, outdoor concerts, antiquing, fishing, or hiking? The possibilities are endless when your pet is trained to a carry bag. Just don't make his first afternoon on the town too hectic. He could easily be overwhelmed and frightened by strange people and places. Introduce him to the social scene gradually. The idea is to socialize him, not to scare him.

Here's a word of advice. Your furball may be ready, willing, and able to go anywhere, but he won't be welcome everywhere. Be a responsible pet owner and check in advance. Never try smuggling him into places. There could be unpleasant consequences—and anyway, it's embarrassing if you get caught.

Chapter Fourteen

Have Ferret, Will Travel

Bon voyage!

Basically anywhere you go your ferret will love to tag along. You could probably use a little company on your jaunts around town. And for family visits and vacations, there's no need to bother the neighbors for pet-sitting. Take your ferret with you. Here are some tips that will help make your travels together safe and hassle free.

Public transit

Is public transit your main means of getting around? Check with your local transit office before taking your pet on buses, trolleys, street cars, or the subway. Different cities have different regulations. It's best to get the policy in writing. After all, the worker at the ticket window may not have current ferret facts at her fingertips. Do you prefer taking a taxi? If so, phone the company before you hail a cab.

Always keep your pet in an escape-proof carry bag or travel carrier and show consideration for other passengers. A little ferret head poking out to say hello could cause pandemonium on the bus.

Short trips—buckle up

Do you usually get around in a car? Most ferrets are willing passengers. The basic rule for car travel with a ferret is *never* allow her to wander loose in the car, *ever*. A free-roaming ferret can be a liability to herself, to you, and to others on the road. Think of what could happen if your pet decided to sniff at the brake pedal the moment you needed to stop. Even a parked car is not a good place for ferret rummaging. There are holes for hiding and sneaking, dangers lurking beneath the seats, odds and ends in the ashtray, and thingamajigs under the dash. In short, she has lots to get into.

How do you keep your pet in one place? For short trips around town, you can use a seat restraint. Buy a small coupler at your pet store. Put your ferret into her harness. Latch up the seat belt on the passenger side as if someone were sitting there. Wrap one end of the coupler around the seat belt once or twice. Then attach one of the snap hooks to the coupler's center ring and the other snap hook to your ferret's harness. If this makes the restraint too long, attach both hooks to the harness. This setup allows your frisky friend some freedom of movement, but keeps her in the seat. It is not, however, a safety device.

Before setting out in the car, wait until your pet has used her litter box. There's nothing more annoying than to be a mile from home and have your furball start that litter box dance.

To keep your ferret in his seat, start with a coupler . . .

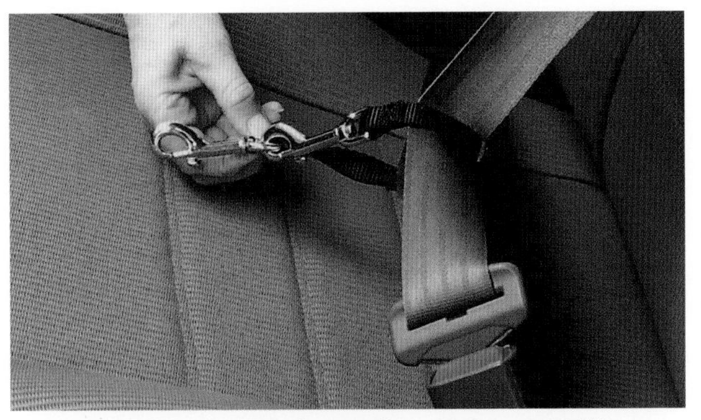

. . . latch the seat belt and wrap the coupler around it . . .

Long hauls

Are you planning a vacation that involves a long car ride? If you can't bear to leave your baby at home, you need to prepare a bit differently for lengthy trips. First, the seat restraint won't do. How could your passenger get at her litter box, food, and water? For long hauls a travel carrier in the back seat is the answer. There are many sizes and styles available. Look for one that fits your car and your budget but is big enough for all your pet's paraphernalia. Some travel carriers are made to be used with a seat belt. This prevents them from flying through the air if the car stops suddenly. For others, loop the car seat belt over the top of the carrier,

. . . hook up your ferret, and you're ready for the road.

through the handle, and then buckle up. Is the seat belt too short? Buy an approved extension.

When you're packing your own suitcase, don't forget to pack one for your ferret's gear. A lock-top plastic storage container, a small diaper bag, or anything similar will do. What should you take?

food for the trip
a water bottle and bottled water
hammock and sleep sack
skin and coat supplement
squeaky toy
zip-lock bag of litter and scoop
plastic bags for droppings
furball medicine
nail clippers and brush
harness and leash
bitter spray
favorite toys
baby wipes and paper towels
health documents

On the trip, an occasional ferret will drive you crazy scratching to get out of her travel carrier. To avoid this, make sure that your ferret's had ample opportunity to explore her portable cage before the journey. Also get her used to car rides well before you travel any distance. She'll be more likely to fall asleep after a good workout, so tire her out before leaving home and let her stretch her legs whenever you stop to stretch your own. Ignore all her scratching, or she'll learn that scratching equals getting out. Most ferrets soon give

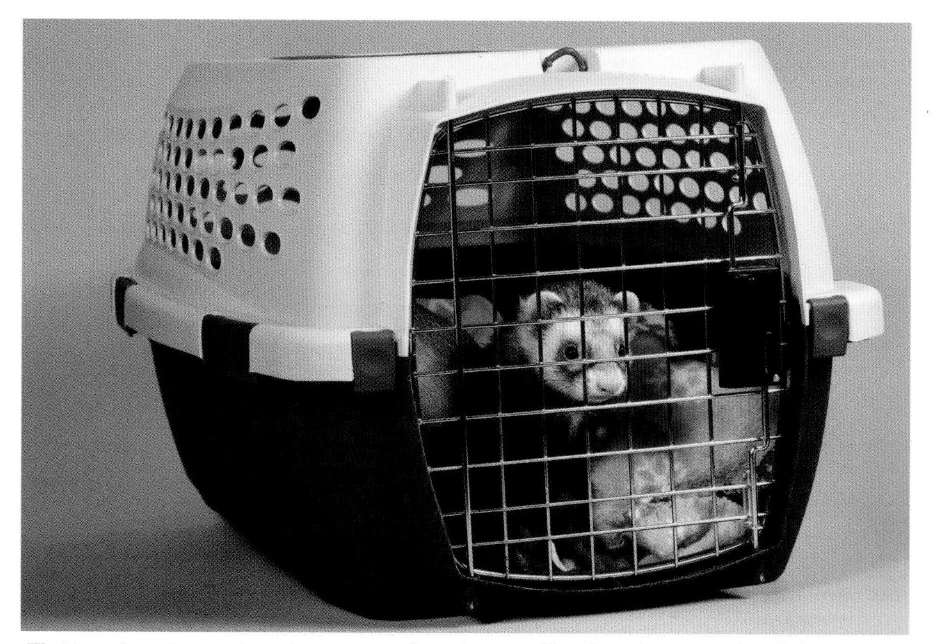

The travel carrier can be a home away from home with a favorite toy and bedding.

up and snooze while you drive. If all else fails, turn the radio up louder (just joking!).

Note of warning: When transporting your pet by car, be aware that whether she's in a pet restraint or in a carrier, there's always a possibility that she could be injured (or worse) if you stop suddenly or are involved in an accident.

Your ferret needs a suitcase, too.

Temperature's rising

Some like it hot, but your ferret does not. In fact, high temperatures in a car during the spring, summer, or fall can be life threatening to your pet. Even a mild day with bright sunshine can turn a car interior into an oven in a matter of minutes.

Never put your ferret into a hot car. Cool it off first by running the air conditioner for a few minutes. No air-conditioning? This presents a big problem. When the weather's hot, you shouldn't be traveling with a ferret in a car without air-conditioning because it doesn't take long for a ferret to experience heatstroke. If, however, you really must take your ferret along with you on a hot day, your best plan is to borrow or rent a car with air-conditioning.

What can you do in an emergency situation (such as a trip to the veterinarian), when you have no option but to use a hot car to transport your pet? Here are some suggestions to try. Install a portable car fan and aim it at your buddy. Wrap hard-sided cold packs in towels or pillowcases and put them next to her. (Avoid the gel packs in plastic bags because your ferret might tear the bag.) If you don't have any cold packs around, improvise! Put ice cubes in plastic food containers or zip-lock bags.

Frequent flyer

Is your pet going to be racking up frequent flyer miles? Better contact the airlines first. Some allow pets. Some do not. Some allow pets in the cabin. Some do not. Ask in advance and get it in writing. You'd be furious if you got to the ticket counter and found out that no one has any idea whether the airline allows those *things* on board.

If your pet is allowed in the cabin with you, you'll need an airline-

After a bedtime workout, this little fuzzy is ready for a good night's sleep.

approved carrier, small enough to fit under the seat. If your ferret isn't allowed in the cabin, think twice about taking her. The cargo section can be too hot or too cold for a ferret. Before leaving, ask your veterinarian for an up-to-date health certificate and for advice on flying with your ferret.

Heartbreak hotel

It's late, you're looking for a motel, and every one has the *No Pets Allowed* sign hanging out front. Do yourself a favor when traveling with your pet—call ahead and make reservations. Otherwise, you might find that there's no room at the inn. Luckily, ferrets don't bark or whine in the middle of the night, so many motels will put out the welcome mat for your well-behaved pet.

Never let your ferret run loose in a motel room. Remember what a tireless explorer she is. Do you think the manager saw to the ferret-proofing before you arrived? Your ferret could easily get under the bed, rip a hole in the box-spring cover, crawl inside, and get caught in the box springs. How do you explain this to the front desk? She could swallow a little something the cleaning staff missed. She could crawl under the dresser and refuse to come out at checkout time. No problem, you think? Just move the dresser and pull her out? That's fine, unless, of course, the furniture is fastened to the wall.

So you can't let her run loose in the room, and you certainly can't keep her confined in her cage the whole time. What's the answer? While at the motel, any playtime should be done on a leash, with the end tied to the travel carrier or held by you.

If you thought scratching was annoying in the car, you'll appreciate it even less in the middle of the night when you want to sleep and your ferret wants to explore. Don't wait until the scratching starts; there's a lot you can do to prevent it. After you've settled into your room, put your pet on her leash and let her snoop around. She can satisfy her curiosity under your watchful eye; then she'll be less likely to bug you at 2:00 A.M. Wear her out before bedtime with a brisk walk and energetic play. March her up and down the corridors; she'll enjoy patrolling the halls. Just look out for foreign objects that could wind up as a midnight snack. If she gets a good enough workout, she'll be glad to get into her cage for some shut-eye. To minimize any disturbance when you're sleeping, park her cage in the bathroom, close the door, and find your earplugs.

The paper trail

Before you set off on your travels together, have all your ferret's documents on hand and up-to-date. Take along her health records, proof of rabies and distemper shots, and a current health certificate issued by an accredited veterinarian.

It's very important for you to know that certain states, cities, and small towns have declared themselves Ferret-Free Zones. Never take your ferret into an FFZ. She could be confiscated, and shipped to a shelter or euthanized. To avoid this possibility, always check with the appropriate authorities before making any travel plans. Are you planning to cross international borders? Call months in advance and ask for information in writing. Import permits may be necessary to take your gad-about across borders or to get her back home.

If you want a warm welcome

Don't take your pet along uninvited. Please ask first. Just because you love your ferret doesn't mean that Uncle Ray and Aunt Margie will, even if you've named your darling after one of them!

Chapter Fifteen
Sitting Pretty

Smile for the camera

Is it family portrait time? If you want your ferret to sit up and smile for the camera, you'll have to teach him how. Well, maybe not the smiling part, but he can be taught to sit. And it's pretty easy. In fact, it's probably the easiest training so far. Of course, he won't sit on command like a dog. You can say, "Patch, sit!" until you're blue in the face, and he'll go on his merry way regardless. But grab those ferret treats, read on, and you'll have your ferret "sitting pretty" in no time.

Trick for treat

Striking a picture-perfect pose comes naturally to most ferrets. They just don't *know* they can do it. That's where you come in. First,

Sitting up is easy to teach. Put a treat by your ferret's nose . . .

. . . gradually raise the treat so he sits up to get it . . .

clear the decks for action so that your pet's not distracted. Then pick one of his favorite treats. Put it right in front of his nose and say, "Patch, sit!" Raise the treat up, tempting him to follow it until he's sitting on his haunches. Then give him the reward and lots of praise. Repeat this three or four times at a "sitting," several times a day. Don't let him cheat! He's wily enough to try leaning on the nearest chair, cupboard, or knee. Or, he might try grabbing the goodie.

. . . then give a reward.

Hitching a ride

Are those little legs tired? Are you halfway home from the park and your buddy needs a break? Hitching a ride on your shoulder could be the answer. Some ferrets have no trouble with a balancing act. Others, however, need a bit of encouragement. So, it's good old treat time again. Get a special one ready and perch your ferret comfortably on your shoulder. While you walk around the house, let him nibble or lick the tidbit from your finger. Be careful, though! Don't let him fall or jump off. The goal is to keep him on your shoulder for progressively longer periods of time. Talk softly to your pet and stroke his head. After he gets the hang of things, he should be happy to ride there without putting a dent in the treat supply.

No head for heights?

Do you have a scaredy cat who doesn't appreciate a bird's-eye view? He might feel safer on your shoulder if you start by sitting rather than standing. Or, you might try waiting until he's a little older and not quite so frisky. Speaking of frisky, if he's really squirmy, it may be litter box time.

Some ferrets are just not shoulder sitters. If yours falls into this category, don't force him. Try the front pouch of a sweatshirt instead. It's better to have a happy ferret than a hurt ferret.

Patch sitting on Andrew's shoulder . . .

Hood-winks

That scaredy cat who won't sit on your shoulder might be happy to hole up in the hood of your sweat-shirt or coat. This is another popular means of ferret transportation. Training to a hood can be a little more difficult than to the shoulder. The technique is the same, but, because you don't have eyes in the back of your head, it's hard to know what your baby's up to. Beware of a bail out! Another pair of hands could be helpful during training to prevent a fall. Once he's happily hunkered down in your hood, he'll most likely catch forty winks.

Another use for the clicker?

Are you and your fuzzy hooked on clicker training? If so, grab your clicker and get to work! A fuzzy who knows that *click* equals treat will be sitting pretty and riding on your shoulder in no time.

. . . and hitching a ride in his hood.

Chapter Sixteen
Stay Out of Those Houseplants

Green thumbs, beware

For all you houseplant enthusiasts (and who isn't?), here's a word of warning—ferrets love wet soil. With just one whiff of that delectable aroma, damp earth, your furry friend will be off and running—where's the plant, where's the plant, where's the plant? And when she reaches her goal, will your ferret be content to smell the flowers or admire the foliage? Not on your life! For your ferret, pay dirt means play dirt.

Ferrets love to dig and tunnel. Your houseplants provide a convenient outlet for this obsession. Apart from the mess digging can cause, it can be detrimental to the health of your plants. Even worse, some plants can be hazardous to the health of your ferret. If your kit gets into a dieffenbachia, for example, she could be poisoned. Stinky's owner spent hundreds of dollars in veterinary bills after his determined digger got at a dieffenbachia.

On page 88 is a list of the more common plants that can be toxic to house pets. If you have any of these

"Where's the plant, where's the plant, where's the plant?"

Hazardous Plants

acalypha	cyclamen	narcissus
ageratum	dieffenbachia	natal palm
allamanda	elephant ear	oleander
amaryllis	English ivy	ornamental pepper
anthurium	eucalyptus	petunia
aucuba	euphorbia	philodendron
autumn crocus	heliotrope	poinsettia
azalea	holly	primrose
bird-of-paradise	honeysuckle	pyracantha
boxwood	hoya	sago palm
browallia	hyacinth	senecio
brunfelsia	hydrangea	spider plant
burro's tail	iris	star jasmine
calla lily	jasmine	sweet pea
castor bean	Jerusalem cherry	Swiss cheese plant
Chinese evergreen	lantana	tulip
clivia	lily of the valley	wax begonia
croton	mistletoe	

plants, put them well out of your ferret's reach. It's always better to play it safe.

Soil-saving solutions

The best way to guarantee that your ferret won't get into your houseplants is to remove the plants from your ferret's reach, by hanging them from ceiling hooks or relocating them to a ferret-free room. Another possibility is to place your plants on an inaccessible shelf, table, or plant stand. But, make sure

Wire mesh and landscape stones keep plants safe from ferret attacks.

that the shelf, table, or plant stand is *really* inaccessible! Many a wily weasel has sneaked up on a plant by a devious route . . . jumping from floor to chair, to table, to plant.

If moving the plant is not possible or practical, then you'll have to cover up the dirt so your ferret can't dig in it. How do you do this? Fit overlapping pieces of galvanized half-inch mesh screening on top of the plant dirt, trimming it to fit with wire cutters. Don't waste your money buying regular window screening that your ferret can easily rip with her claws. Next, cover the screening with landscape stones, two to three inches in diameter. Make the layer of stones at least two inches thick. As an inexpensive alternative, try flat river rocks. Your ferret shouldn't be able to move the stones or rocks. However, if you have a little Amazon, the screening will prevent her from hitting pay dirt. With some plants, the use of screening may not be feasible. In this case, pile up those larger stones as deeply as possible. Where the pot is too small for stones, or can be easily knocked over, find a sunny spot for the plant well out of ferret reach.

A loud, firm "NO!" is in order whenever the little digger goes near a plant—every time . . . always. Consistency is the key. She needs to know you mean business.

Oh, no! Foiled again!

The greenhouse effect

If you try these suggestions, you won't have to find new homes for your plants or sell them off at your next garage sale. Once more, your home can be a green oasis. And you can keep the ferret, too.

Chapter Seventeen

Don't Sweep the Carpet Problem Under the Rug

An itch to scratch?

Carpet clawing by your favorite fuzzy is not only very annoying, but can be quite destructive as well. If your ferret gets obsessive about scratching a certain carpeted corner, you could end up with hardwood floors in no time.

Why do some ferrets *scrraaattchh* at carpets? There are usually two reasons. First, the little rug rat probably wants into a room you have designated off limits. When Chester wants to explore behind a closed door, you can guarantee he'll try to tunnel his way to the other side. This is bad news for your carpet. The second reason for clawing is that Chester wants under something, be it the sofa, the chair, or the TV stand. Ignoring the problem won't make it go away—and a ferret should never be declawed—so here are a few solutions to try.

Scratching to get in?

Redirect that scratch

Every time Chester starts to scratch the carpet, pick him up quickly, say "NO!" loudly and firmly, and move him from the area. Then, direct his attention to something more interesting, such as his toys or his tunnel system. This works for some ferrets—it gets their minds off the carpet and onto playtime. Unfortunately, other ferrets are not so easily distracted, so with them you'll have to take a different approach.

Distract your ferret from destructive behavior...take time out to play with him.

Get a whiff of this

Some ferrets don't like the smell of a bitter spray, let alone the taste. Because you already have a bitter spray around, it doesn't hurt to try it. Spray a little bit on an inconspicuous spot of carpet to test for color fastness; then spray it on the area Chester likes to claw. You'll need to respray the area twice a day so that the smell doesn't dissipate, but don't saturate the carpet. If you're lucky, your ferret will take one sniff and run the other way. Will dog and cat repellent sprays work? They won't work for most ferrets.

Cover up

Short of posting a sentry at the doorway, you may never be able to stop your ferret's scratching. But, you can at least protect the carpet from damage. Purchase a length of clear plastic carpet runner that is about two feet longer than the width of your doorway. Cut it into an H-shape so that it fits snugly around both sides of the door frame and extends about a foot to the left and right of the doorway, as well as about a foot on either side of the threshold. (See photo.) Place it nubby side down and secure all the edges to the carpet with duct tape. Don't miss even a fraction of an inch or the great investigator will find the gap, tear the tape, and wiggle under the plastic. Once you've got the plastic in place, Chester will be scratching at the runner rather than at the rug. The plastic may even discourage his clawing completely.

Ferrets are, however, crafty little creatures. If they can't scratch their way *under* the door, watch them try scratching their way *through* the door. Door scratching is annoying, destructive, and difficult to stop. Try covering the lower part of the door—the part he can reach—with a piece(s) of smooth plastic runner. Tape all four edges securely to the door. If there are any small breaks in the tape, he'll be able to rip everything off. A smear of bitter spray or cream on the plastic will prevent him from tearing at it with his teeth. Whenever you do catch him storming the door, say "NO!" and scoot him to his play area. What happens when you're too late and he's already made his mark? Painted doors can easily be retouched, and any scratches in stained woodwork can be camouflaged with brown shoe polish or liquid scratch cover.

This is how to fit a piece of plastic carpet runner into a doorway to prevent your ferret from scratching the carpet when the door is closed.

Doorways aren't the only place you may find Chester digging. After you've ferret-proofed the sofa, he may have lingering memories of his cozy nest underneath. Months later, he'll still be scratching to worm his way in. Discourage him by using plastic, tape, and spray, as already described, or use an electrostatic pet mat.

Keep off!

Electrostatic pet mats can be found at your local pet supply store, or ordered from the Internet. These vinyl mats come in various sizes, and are effective training aids recognized by humane societies and veterinary associations. They will keep your pet away from a particular spot or hazard when nothing else will. How do they work? They have embedded wires that are powered by a battery/AC power pack. When

Carpet isn't the only flooring a ferret will target. Linoleum comes under attack, too.

your pet walks on a mat, he'll be surprised by a tingling sensation similar to static electricity. The mats are quite harmless, but they get the message across—keep off!

Before using one of these mats with ferrets, read the instructions carefully. Then remove and discard the rubberized pads from the bottom of the power pack, as well as the cover for the AC adapter connection that you'll find on the side of the pack. If you don't remove these rubbery pieces, your ferret could tear them off and eat them.

Placement of the mat depends on what you're trying to protect. If Chester's wrecking the rug, place a mat on top of the problem area. If he's scratching on a door, place a mat in front of the door. In either case, secure the mat with duct tape to prevent your furball from crawling underneath. The first time you turn on the mat, start out on the lowest setting and watch what happens. When Chester steps on the mat, he should quickly back off. If he doesn't, adjust the intensity setting on the power pack.

Carpet shark

Does your ferret love to glide through the carpet, nose first? Don't use powdered carpet deodorizers or cleaners. These can irritate little chins, eyes, noses, and lungs. So scrap these powders and let your ferret surf safely through the rug like a true carpet shark!

Chapter Eighteen

Odds 'n' Ends

Company's coming

Are friends coming for the weekend? When a ferret's part of your family, you'll have to worry about more than the menu and the sleeping arrangements. Every guest visit is a golden opportunity for your busybody. She'll be quick to take advantage of a door left open, a cupboard ajar, a bag lying on the floor. Any open suitcase will be an open invitation to snoop. Your ferret's not particular. She'll steal from the guests just as happily as she does from you. Cosmetic sponges, slippers, mittens, kid's toys, medication—the list of possibilities goes on and on.

New toes could be a tempting new target for your ferret to nibble. So when you're bringing out the drinks, why not bring out the bitter spray, too, and ferret-proof those exposed toes? And visitors don't think about watching their step, so make sure that they don't step on your ferret. For safety's sake, she may have to spend more time in her cage. The bottom line is—be alert when company comes. And be considerate. You may love your little cutie, but your company may not appreciate ferret kisses.

Cache and carry

Or is it carry and cache? Caching is an instinct in ferrets. You can't really control this behavior. No matter what you do, the little pack rat will keep stashing away stolen treasures. You'll be surprised what can wind up in her secret collection—remote controls, pliers, toys, can coolers, hairbrushes, extension cords. Have you misplaced your keys? Check your ferret's stockpile. Does she do a hit-and-run on her food bowl—grab a mouthful and speed off to her hoard? You'll have to remove the food hidden in her personal pantry so that it doesn't turn moldy.

Ho! Ho! Ho! HELP!

Christmas is loads of fun for a ferret. Look at it from her point of view. You've just put out all sorts of wonderful new toys—the stockings at the fireplace, the table decorations, the swagged garlands on the banis-

Holiday decorations should be kept out of ferret reach.

ter, your heirloom nativity scene, and your number-one holiday headache with a ferret, the Christmas tree.

A real Christmas tree is just an overgrown houseplant to your pet—only better! There's the earthy smell, sticky sap, water to drink, and branches to climb. An artificial tree is just as bad. It also has balls to swat, tinsel to steal, light cords to test, and piles of presents underneath.

The easiest solution for a no-hassle Christmas is to keep the room with the tree off limits for the holiday season. If that isn't possible, tie the tree to something sturdy close by, use only plain water in the stand, cut off all low-hanging branches, hang ornaments and tinsel well out of ferret reach, rub a bitter gel or cream on light cords, and keep presents locked away until the big day.

Or, if you like your tree the way it was last year, use an electrostatic pet mat or two. Secure the mat(s) to the floor with duct tape, or the little sneak will tunnel her way under and hit those presents pronto. Remove any low-trailing branches, or she'll be smart enough to use one as a bridge over the mat. Does the idea of using an electrostatic pet mat ruffle your feathers? Just remember that it's much better for your pet to experience a slight, static pulse than to have a tree crash down around her ears.

Christmas isn't the only holiday when extra decorations come out of storage. Don't forget Hanukkah, Easter, Fourth of July, Valentine's Day, St. Patrick's Day, and Halloween. Curious ferrets can have a field day on these holidays, too. The same goes for birthday parties. Watch out for the balloons, candles, and goodie bags.

Tips

The following tips are not really training hints, but they could help make life easier with your ferret. Are you having trouble cleaning ears or cutting nails? A few drops of skin and coat supplement or a dab of vitamin paste on her tummy will keep your pet occupied while you take care of business. Most ferrets love to have their ears rubbed, so sneak in a cleaning while you massage. Or, try to do the grooming when she's fast asleep.

During the twice-yearly coat change, shedding can be controlled

A lost ferret doesn't have a homing instinct. If your pet gets out of the house, you'll have to go looking for her.

by using a small-toothed flea comb or a grooming mitt. Or, pluck your pal. Holding her over a newspaper, quickly tug out little bits of fur from all over her body. This is a fast and effective way to remove shedding hair, and it won't hurt your ferret one bit.

Does your ferret stubbornly clamp her jaws shut when it's time for medicine? Mix it with a little skin and coat supplement or vitamin paste, and she'll lap it right up.

Lost ferret

Ferrets are always looking for adventure and, even if you're very careful, escapes can happen. If your ferret slips away, organize a search party immediately and then get outside and squeak that squeaky toy all over your yard. No luck? Place her cage outside with fresh food and water. Fluff up her bedding and lay a trail of coat supplement drops to the cage. Check with neighbors; then fan out and squeak around the neighborhood. Still no luck? Call the Humane Society and ferret organizations in your area, nail up flyers and posters as quickly as possible, and check the lost-and-found services offered by your local newspaper and radio stations.

If your ferret's wearing a collar or harness with a bell and identification tag, anyone finding her will know she's a pet, and you'll have a much better chance of a speedy reunion. As an added safeguard, you could take your ferret to her veterinarian to see about microchip identification.

Chapter Nineteen

Reaping Your Reward

Top of the class

Now your ferret has graduated from training, ideally with honors! Your hard work has paid off, and the instruction time has been minimal when you consider the benefits. Gone are the days of chasing your kit out of the cupboards or the houseplants. Now you can devote your energies to having fun together. You won't have to waste time anymore searching under beds, in closets, or behind furniture for a mislaid pet. Instead, you can have instant ferret by calling his name or squeaking for him. No longer will you have to leave him home alone or bother Auntie Barbara to pet sit. He's now the perfect traveling companion.

Continuing education

Training is an ongoing job; you don't want your student backsliding after all your good work together. So always keep up the reminders and the rewards. In the end, it's your commitment and dedication that will give your ferret the opportunity to become the best pet he can be . . . and that is a pretty wonderful pet!

Training is an ongoing job. Keep up the reminders and the rewards.

Useful Addresses and Literature

Ferret organizations and web sites

Because ferret organizations often dissolve or restructure, please visit *www.ferretcentral.org/orgs.html* and/or *www.weaselwords.com/page/links_clubs.php* for current state, provincial, national, and international listings.

The American Ferret Association (AFA)
Phone: 1-888-FERRET-1
Web site: *www.ferret.org*
E-Mail: *afa@ferret.org*

Ferret Central
Web site: *www.ferretcentral.org*

Ferret Family Services
Phone: (785) 456-8337
Web site: *www.ferretfamilyservices.org*
E-mail: *sprite@ksu.edu*

Ferret Information Rescue Shelter FIRST (Ferret) Society
British Columbia, Canada
Phone: (604) 263-7481
E-mail: first@ferrets.org

There are literally hundreds of local ferret clubs and associations throughout the world. Check the Internet for an organization near you. And, don't forget the abandoned ferrets that are looking for a good home. Again, search the Internet for a shelter near you where you can adopt a fuzzy or become a volunteer.

Books

Complete Guide to Ferrets
James McKay
Swan Hill Press, 2002

Ferret (Caring for Your Pet)
Lynn Hamilton
Weigl Publishers, 2000

Ferrets
Animal Planet Pet Care Library
Vickie McKimmey
TFH Publications, 2007

Ferrets: Complete Care Guide
Karen Dale Dustman
BowTie Press, 2002

Ferrets (Complete Pet Owner's Manual)
E. Lynn Morton
Barron's Educational Series, Inc., 2000

Ferrets for Dummies, 2nd edition
Kim Shilling
For Dummies, 2007

Find Out About Ferrets: The Complete Guide to Turning Your Ferret Into the Happiest, Best-Behaved and Healthiest Pet in the World!
Colin Patterson
Lulu.com, 2006

The Ferret Handbook
Gerry Bucsis and Barbara Somerville
Barron's Educational Series, Inc., 2001

The Simple Guide to Ferrets
Bobbye Land
TFH Publications, 2003

Your Outta Control Ferret
Bobbye Land
TFH Publications, 2003

500 Things My Ferret Told Me
Mary R. Shefferman
Modern Ferret Magazine, 2002

Clicker training (CT) is an effective method of training ferrets. You can adapt the CT techniques that are used to train dogs, birds, and horses to train your ferret. There are too many CT books to list here, so please check the Internet or your local bookstore for books that interest you.

Periodicals

FerretsMagazine.com
An online magazine for ferret owners by BowTie Press

Ferrets USA
Annual magazine by BowTie Press

Miscellaneous

The Essential Guide to Caring For Your Pet Ferret
Pet Video Library Books on Video
Small Animal Series
DVD

The Pursuit of Excellence: Ferrets
PBS Home Video
DVD

Index

Fun-loving
Energetic
Rambunctious
Rewarding
Endearing
Trainable